Emerging Elders

Emerging Elders

Developing Shepherds in God's Image

Ron Clark

LEAFWOOD
PUBLISHERS
Abilene, TX

EMERGING ELDERS:
Developing Shepherds in God's Image

Copyright 2008 by Ron Clark

ISBN 978-0-89112-569-3

Printed in the United States of America

Scripture quotations, unless otherwise noted, are from The Holy Bible,
New International Version. Copyright 1984, International Bible Society.
Used by permission of Zondervan Publishers.

Cover design by Mark Decker
Interior text design by Sandy Armstrong
Author photo by www.2ndsunphoto.com

For information contact:
Leafwood Publishers, Abilene, Texas
1-877-816-4455 toll free
www.leafwoodpublishers.com

08 09 10 11 12 13 14 / 7 6 5 4 3 2 1

CONTENTS

Preface 7

Introduction 9

SECTION 1: Why Elder Development? 19

1. Do We Need Elders? 21

2. Shepherds and Growing Flocks 33

SECTION 2: Good Shepherds 43

3. The Lord is My Shepherd:
   How God Models Leadership 45

4. Baaaaaad Shepherds:
   Dysfunctional Leadership in the Kingdom 65

5. Elders and the Spirit 81

6. Elders and Their Families 93

7. Elders Reflect the Nature of Christ 103

8. Shepherding for Evangelism through Discipleship 111

SECTION 3: Issues Facing Today's Good Shepherds 123

9. Developing Faith in the Members 125

10. Promoting Unity in the Body of Christ 133

11. Shepherding Dysfunctional Families 143

12. Shepherding the Congregation:
    Who Are the Real Predators? 151

13. Shepherding Ministers 163

14. The Future of Shepherding 177

15. Suggested Elder Development Program 185

Endnotes 191

Acknowledgements 205

PREFACE

The business world churns out books and resources on leadership. Our churches followed suit. I saw motivational movie clips and presentations using McDonald's, Wal-Mart, and the flying fish market in Seattle. All were valiant attempts to help our churches think about leadership and cultivate an environment to develop future leaders. I am thankful for this work because it started a process of thinking and research on leadership in my ministry. During this movement I began to devour books by Lynn Anderson, Ian Fair, Robert Clinton, John Maxwell, and Warren Bennis. I read them over and over and had our leaders buy them for leadership classes. These were excellent resources and many wonderful discussions came from these books.

We face a dilemma. In the Churches of Christ and other Restoration churches we use a different system. The corporate makeovers of churches may work if the preacher is the CEO, but God empowered leaders to work together, as a team, and in support of each other. I continued to see the criticism of Anderson's and Fair's books by elders as possibly leading to division in leadership. It seems that elders and ministers were once again struggling over who was and should be in control. In addition to this, I'm finding myself more a pastor who hears the cries of neglected sheep.

On top of all this, we are losing people from our churches. The population of unchurched people is growing faster than the churches. We are outnumbered and still fighting about who is in charge. There has to be a better way.

In my work with spousal and sexual abuse and social justice the evidence continues to mount—men have power issues and we need to work together to empower the next generation to reflect the compassion, empathy, mercy, and love of Jesus. In a word, we need leaders who act like Jesus to bring young people back to church. Young people from dysfunctional and abusive homes suffer and resist relationships. These young people need to see the gentleness of Jesus in the lives of leaders so that they can call God Father with a smile and security. They need compassionate shepherds.

In the leadership literature the question is asked, "Are people born leaders or do we train them to become leaders?" I suggest a third option. *Leaders emerge.* When we begin to offer training and development ministries, *leaders emerge.* They become visible because we help them address issues and strengthen their skills. When we focus on compassion, empathy, and mercy they emerge because they desire to reflect these morals.

When the pressure is on and the church begins to grow, *leaders emerge.* They emerge because they are fed and they want to step up to the task. They see that the church cares about people and they rise up. When the early church was persecuted the leaders were targeted. Yet, there were always people to take their place. When violence reigns, people know that compassion and mercy must continue so that we might win the battle.

When God's image needs to be manifested, *leaders emerge.* God places people of compassion in leadership because that is how the glory of God is displayed. God leads and guides leaders to shine because they reflect the glory of Jesus. So *leaders emerge* and they manifest the image of God. They emerge because God places them forward. They manifest God's image because that is how God plans to transform our world.

INTRODUCTION

In my experiences as a graduate student, teacher, and minister, I have noticed that, in the Churches of Christ, few books are written specifically for ministers about our style of ministry. In the Churches of Christ and Christian Churches, we attempt to let the Bible be our guide in our personal walk with Jesus, as well as our model for congregational growth, ministry, and leadership. Robert Richardson, one of our early leaders in the American branch of the Restoration Movement, said that our ministry style is unique because evangelists and pastors are two distinct positions in the church.

> The Lord Jesus Christ, the great Shepherd of the flock, has committed the care of his church to pastors, or under-shepherds, who are commanded to "feed the flock of God," taking the oversight thereof, not by constraint, but willingly; not for filthy lucre, but of a ready mind. In the Scriptures, pastors are sometimes called bishops, or overseers, from the fact that they are usually possessed of age and experiences . . . Evangelists or missionaries are also sustained by the churches, in the work of preaching the gospel to the world.[1]

We, as a movement, are unique to many churches and denominations because, as Richardson suggests, we believe that Jesus has appointed elders to pastor the church and evangelists to preach. Many other churches have the preacher/pastor system: the preacher is usually the senior pastor and is not only the main voice for the congregation but may also have authority over any other existing leadership committee. In the book *Who's in Charge? Four Church Leader Models*, one view suggests the preacher is one of the pastors/elders. The main emphasis of this pastor is that he is a teaching elder. Other ministers can become pastors/elders of the church. Some Emergent churches also use the senior pastor/elder model. Church plants use the title lead church planter, senior minister, or preaching pastor. This does produce a different dynamic than those functioning with evangelists and elders. These churches believe that they are led by God but also driven by the senior minister's vision, calling, and direction.

While many books on congregational ministry have been written to help these pastors become ranchers, facilitators, respected CEOs, or servants, the fact remains that these individuals carry a respect and authority that sometimes is missing in the Restoration churches. I know of preachers who abuse their power, and I know of preachers who use their authority to empower their churches to grow and witness God's love in their communities. The senior ministers that I know in these churches have shared with me that they carry a great responsibility, many times alone, and that what they preach from the pulpit usually becomes the guiding vision and authority in the lives of those who attend or visit their congregations. Other leaders have a deep respect for these senior ministers and trust that they carry God's vision for the church. While missional and emergent churches suggest that leadership is decentralized and tend to avoid a hierarchical system of leadership, they do embrace the senior minister concept, although they may use different terminology. Research on North American mega churches suggests that the founding minister is so respected that the church's mission and vision reflects his personality and mission for Christ.[2]

Yet, how are we in the Restoration Movement unique in leadership? Preachers and ministers work with elders. Now you may be on the floor laughing at the irony of preachers and elders working together. Or you may think I am being sarcastic and starting to complain. Others may feel that my statement is an expression of relief because we have another group to do the "dirty work" of ministry. Maybe your ministry reflects how you interpret my statement. Our elders, rather than our preachers, are called to be pastors. Elders are the bishops and pastors of the church while the preachers are the evangelists or ministers for the congregation (Acts 20:28; Titus 1:6-7; 1 Peter 5:1-5; Eph. 4:11-12). Our ministers are not to be pastors, but evangelists. While some elders preach *and* shepherd (1 Tim. 5:17), we do acknowledge that these two ministries have different functions. However, both leadership positions have authority from God, and both are necessary for a church to grow and become healthy.

A few years ago, my wife and I were part of a neighborhood Bible study in Portland. Some of the families in our neighborhood would get together to pray for the neighbors, visit, and have a Bible study. We were from different age groups and different churches. They called me Pastor Ron in spite of my encouragement that "Ron is fine." My next door neighbor was an elder in a Presbyterian church near us. One night he asked why I was hesitant about the title "Pastor." I had the group turn to 1 Peter 5, and we talked about how the Apostle Peter, an elder, used the terms "pastor" and "bishop" for the elders of the church. I also briefly explained the difference between elders and ministers. I shared how our church tried to practice this concept. One of the other couples mentioned that the preacher was the senior pastor in their church and that the elders were simply a board, appointed by him and needed for financial and corporate issues. It became a lively discussion. My next door neighbor quietly listened and said he understood.

The next day he came to me and said that he had been looking at that text and realized something about his role as an elder. He felt that their pastor could be out in the community if the elders were encouraged to shepherd more and relieve the minister of that responsibility. It was a good discussion on my front porch that ended with both of us feeling a sense of accomplishment. A few weeks later my neighbor said that the pastor was not interested in delegating that responsibility to the elders and had encouraged them to continue as they had been. Two years later, my neighbor passed away. When we visited his wife, we talked about the neighborhood study, his role as an elder, and his desire to do more. About a year later she told me that she had been appointed one of the three elders in that church. I asked, "What does an elder do in your church?"

"I don't know," she said.

Preachers need to be free to preach and focus on evangelism. Elders also should not be relegated to be a board of directors. Not that this is bad in itself, but it is a matter of giftedness. Preachers have a gift to preach, call the congregation to holiness and courage, inspire the weak and oppressed, and challenge the evil forces and power structures in the community to seek God. We are called to go into the community and bring the gospel to those seeking God. We have authority from God to fulfill this role (2 Tim. 4:5). While we may also visit, encourage, and shepherd, our efforts can focus on outreach.

Elders, on the other hand, are appointed by the Holy Spirit to be bishops (overseers) and shepherds (pastor) of Christ's sheep (Acts 20:28). The Spirit empowers elders to do this task. They are to pray for the sick (James 5:14), protect the flock (Acts 20:28; 1 Peter 5:1-5), and seek and save the lost (Luke 15). While elders may do community outreach, their giftedness is pastoral. Yet, so often I am told that preachers have a pastoral function. Possibly, but our main work is not to shepherd; that is the task of elders and their wives who have been called by God. Elders and their wives can use their gifts to nurture the church.

We each have authority, by God, based on our giftedness. Elders and evangelists work together to guide the church to growth, unity, and spiritual maturity (Eph. 4:11-16). Shepherding is not a dirty job; it is a divine calling. While it is hard work, it brings great reward. Peter told the elders that Jesus (their chief shepherd) will give them an unfading crown of glory. This crown of glory is the one given to martyrs and those who die in persecution. Elders who shepherd their congregations, as Jesus desires, do have a wonderful reward.

I was speaking to a group of ministers and elders about our elder development ministry. One elder said that I was forgetting that ministers had a "pastoral" function, too. I said, "Sometimes they do, but the Bible teaches that elders, not ministers, are to pastor the flock." He replied that if ministers weren't expected to visit patients in hospitals, the elderly, and those in the nursing homes, then what were they expected to do? I said, "I do visitation, but it is not my main responsibility. I do this because I am a full-time minister and may be able to get to the hospital the quickest. But God intends for ministers to be involved in the community by teaching and preaching to those looking for Jesus. Our focus is evangelism." The man shook his head as if to say, "Preachers need to be about more important things."

Sometimes churches tend to focus inward. Rather than pushing our preachers to focus their ministry on the community, we in the church expect them to take care of our needs. We expect them to visit those in hospitals, the sick, and those confined to their houses because we feel this is more important than outreach. It seems as if American churches are guilty of narcissism. Do we hire evangelists/preachers to focus on our needs or the needs of the community? More importantly, what has God called our ministers to do? What has God called our elders to do?

I believe that there has been a great struggle in the history of our churches between elders and ministers. Some elders, like my neighbor, are not encouraged by their minister to shepherd the flock. Some elders shepherd the flock but neglect to shepherd the minister and his family. Other elders simply have it in for preachers and feel "you have to live with 'em because you can't live without 'em." The same is true for ministers. Some begin their preaching careers with resentment for elders due to situations they observed in churches or have experienced in their own lives. Some preachers have power issues and resent any group questioning their *authority*. Others develop a long-lasting relationship with elders and have an effective ministry. Congregations also struggle with whether the elders or the ministers should set the direction and vision for the church. One elder indicated that sometimes elders assume that they have all authority in the church, but they have no method to display how their gifts of leadership are practiced. Congregations witness power struggles between elders and ministers and end up being forced to choose sides. One minister told me that much of the energy in their leadership had been used to find out "who was in charge." In these situations no one wins, especially God.

As a minister I acknowledge that I have been pastoral in my ministry for over twenty years. I know that members have felt that I, like many other ministers, have been more of a shepherd than the elders. I also have seen the tension in my own ministry between shepherding and being in the community encouraging people to walk with Jesus. At times I have become addicted to shepherding because I tend to be a rescuer and have at times displayed the "Messiah Complex"—the belief that one person other than Jesus can solve all problems. Shepherding is a rewarding ministry and my desire is that all elders can experience this joy. I also desire that ministers can experience the joy of reaching the lost and empowering our communities to transform in the image of God.

We in the Restoration Movement are unique. Not only is our leadership unique, but we have also been considered by our own church historians to be one of the most divisive and divided movements in American Christianity.[3] We've tried accepting the senior pastor concept by using terms such as senior minister, pulpit minister, or evangelistic oversight. As a church planter I have come to see that this can be effective in helping a church grow. It also provides the church with one single guiding vision and focus on outreach. However, I miss working with elders and having these mature spiritual couples lead small groups and home communities. Lori and I dislike having to spiritually discipline by ourselves. I also see how many of those who visit the new church and come from Restoration backgrounds feel it is their responsibility to question a church with a single authority figure.

Sometimes we go to the extreme by humbling the minister and treating him like a servant-boy. We've confined elders to board rooms, deacon's duties, or decision making. Sometimes we've delayed appointing elders, claiming it is better to be sheep without a shepherd than to have shepherds who are immature and spiritually undeveloped. We've burdened the preacher by expecting their time to be consumed with shepherding, or we've neglected our own wounded. We've convinced ourselves that preachers are paid and therefore can handle the work, even though they are not called to shepherd. Imagine sheep wandering in the wilderness with only a spokesman as a guide.

We have planted churches with preachers and put off elder development for years. We have encouraged ministers and ministry teams to lead churches for a decade with very little thought about developing elders. Our problem is sometimes solved on the mission field. Our preachers and elders are separated by an ocean and thousands of miles, and they only visit every two years, if ever. We have found a way to exist in peace by not speaking. What a disturbing commentary for a movement that began with a desire to unite and promote unity!

I believe that this problem exists for two reasons. First, *we need more literature written to ministers in our movement.* Most of the ministry classes I have taken and taught involve textbooks from churches that call their preachers "senior pastors." While these books have tremendous value in helping our ministers preach, teach, and become evangelistic, they cannot teach them how to work with elders. How many of our preachers are taught the value of, need for, and method of an ongoing elder development program in our churches, church plants, and missions? Some churches in in the Restoration Movement continue to see the preacher as the senior pastor and respect what he has to say, but they need to see the elders also as vibrant leaders in the kingdom. The minister becomes overloaded with the emotional connection to the church and struggles to become a prophet to the kingdom and community where he lives. The visitation and pastoral expectations dominate his schedule and he, in effect, becomes a pastor. The minister's wife lives in his shadow and silently watches him carry a burden alone. She also may carry an emotional burden alone without having deep emotional connections with other women in the church. The churches stagnate and cease to grow because the leaders are not using their gifts. The elders feel unused and simply become older deacons or a board of directors. Elders' wives see themselves as only a "necessary qualification" for their husband and yet fail to enjoy a rewarding ministry to Christian women. We need to train our ministers to work with elders so that they can develop their skills as evangelists.

Second, *we have pumped a tremendous amount of resources into training ministers and very little into training elders.* While we plant preacher training schools in countries throughout the world, we do not give the same thought to elder development programs in those countries. Rarely do we train preachers to develop elders. We also seem to appoint elders as an afterthought. It seems that elders are not seen as an integral part of the growth of a congregation; they are seen as those who keep house. Sometimes I hear that elders are viewed as the ones who take control and kill the momentum of a church or ministry. Somehow elders are often viewed as those who kill a good ministry. I have seen many more elders earn the respect and love of the congregation and their community. Fortunately, there are programs that are now training elders to be more effective. Hope Network and Elderlink (from Abilene Christian University) are targeting elders and their wives and presenting key issues for their growth and development.

    This book is a reworking of my doctoral dissertation on elder development. I have always been under the impression that a big part of my job as a preacher is to train and develop couples to serve as shepherds. Maybe this came from my years as an Eagle Scout working with the outstanding leadership development program that the Boy Scouts of America provide for youth. Maybe it came from my years of being in the presence of evangelists from the mutual ministry movement and seeing their strong emphasis on training others to teach, speak, and lead. Maybe it came from all the stories I have heard about preacher/elder power struggles and how those keep us from growing as we should. Maybe it came from a belief that the biblical outline for church leadership is good and can help a church be the best it can be. Even though in my ministry those who have frustrated me the most have been elders, I still believe in this system of church leadership. As a church planter I see the results of working with people who are committed to a single vision for the church and appreciate not having to argue with leaders over outreach and evangelism. However, I see the need for having shepherding couples in a church that reaches those who have little or no knowledge of Jesus and the Way.

    This book can be used to train elders and their wives, identify emerging leaders, and strengthen elders and ministers in their work. I hope that this makes us more effective and more balanced in our congregational ministries. I also hope that it will develop emerging leaders to lead emerging churches in a post-modern/post-Christian world. Those who use this book will be sent back to the Bible to restudy the texts for personal growth and spiritual development.

Chapter 1 explains my rationale for developing elders. Chapter 2 discusses the development of the office of elder and how this aids churches in growth. I believe that elder development should be a primary focus for a minister and the church, along with outreach and evangelism. Rather than seeking a leadership model in our society I find that elders can begin with a model that is centered in God. Chapters 3, 4, and 5 provide another look at the biblical texts from the view of using them for spiritual growth, development, and future leadership selection. Chapters 6, 7, and 8 provide a working model for ministers and elders and contrast this with dysfunctional leadership. Chapters 9 through 15 provide a suggested outline and topics to address in beginning an elder development program in a church.

My desire is that this book helps elders return to the text and become the elders that God has called them to be. I also hope that congregations will begin their own development ministries in order to provide the church of the future with candidates who are prepared to shepherd the flock so that the ministers can be evangelists in their churches, communities, and the world.

QUESTIONS _____

1. How are the Restoration Movement churches unique in leadership?

2. Why is it important to make a distinction between ministry as evangelism and ministry as pastoral?

3. In your opinion, have we neglected elder development? Why or why not?

4. What are some ways in which you believe elders can be better developed for service in the future?

SECTION ONE

WHY ELDER DEVELOPMENT?

Chapter 1

Do We Need Elders?

Church growth statistics suggest that seventy-five percent of all churches have less than one hundred adult members and sixty percent of all churches have less than one hundred members.[4] This statistic is fairly accurate for Restoration Movement churches. While the Churches of Christ may have a higher number of smaller churches with attendance under one hundred, the growth of the Christian Churches and International Churches would offset these numbers and bring the Restoration Movement statistics in line with the national average. Many smaller churches function without elders. Just as churches need preachers, so churches need elders. Churches need pastors to shepherd the sheep and evangelists/ministers to lead the proclamation of the good news of Jesus. Preachers also need pastors to shepherd their families.

All of the congregations I know of without elders would like to have them. Ministers tell me they wish they had elders. Congregations say they would like to have elders. Yet these churches continue to exist year after year without them. It is almost as if they believe they can't have what they want, or do they consider elders a luxury? Some say they can't find elders. Others say that the qualified ones are too old. Potential elders tell me that they don't know if they can carry the "burden" of leading the church. Others are afraid to take the position because they fear the criticism. It is an awesome and holy task, but it is not an impossible one. Unfortunately, we quit looking and place the burden on the preacher who says, "I'm full time, I might as well do it."

What is our solution? We train and expect ministers to preach and pastor the congregations. In our ministry training, we encourage them to fulfill both roles while avoiding burnout. I haven't found a good book in our movement that teaches ministers how to appoint, work with, and develop elders in the congregation. In some of our preacher training schools and Bible colleges we use ministry resources from churches where the minister is the senior pastor. We either try to adapt the texts to our theology, or we tell ministers that they need to find a way to balance evangelism and pastoral care. The ministers become bogged down with shepherd's work. While they develop a close connection with the members, they are doing two ministries.

I teach classes at George Fox Evangelical Seminary in Portland. Almost all of my students are working in ministry while attending school. Within this movement the ministers are the pastors. They also struggle with burnout, Sabbath rest, boundaries, and delegating their tasks to members, common issues in our churches. We are wonderfully unique in that we have elders to shepherd. But we are like other churches in that we as ministers still have not been able to delegate the shepherding to others. Elders/pastors are gifted by God, and it is important that ministers learn to work with them to share the load of ministry. Yet, we continue to struggle.

Evangelistic Oversight

What is the result of this struggle and what have Christians done about this in the past? One response was to develop a method called *evangelistic oversight*. In the Churches of Christ we have had a movement that began in the early 1800s with Elder Ben Franklin, passed to Daniel Somer, continued with W. Carl Ketcherside, and continues to this day. The churches were called Mutual Ministry or Mutual Edification churches in the mid twentieth century. This movement was frustrated by our emphasis on education and production of preachers whose theological language was distant from most people. The leaders in this movement emphasized a Paul and Timothy style of training and developed men as preachers and elders. The evangelists planted congregation and still had some authority with the congregations that had elders. The elders guided the men of the congregation to lead and preach in the individual churches. The elders were developed, ordained, and then taught, preached, and shepherded the congregation.

In the late 1950s and early 1960s, many of these churches declined and later sought out and hired full-time local evangelists.[5] Many of the elders felt that this was the best move for the church since the congregations were declining. Ketcherside, Garrett, and many others warned the elders that they would become less involved as a result and give the work to the "hireling preachers." In my research with these congregations, it was the evangelists who were most resistant to change within the congregations. The elders wanted to reach the members and in many cases led their congregations to finally seek out and hire a full-time local evangelist. I use the term *transition churches* (TC) for these churches because they became churches that transitioned from mutual ministry churches, but still continued to practice many of the mutual ministry teachings and methods of leadership.

In some ways, Ketcherside and Garrett were right. Many of the transition church elders relegated themselves to teaching classes, leading songs, caring for the building and landscaping, and filling the pulpit when the preacher was gone. In some congregations the preaching was only given to "professional speakers" when the regular preacher was out of town. The minister did become more of a senior pastor. Although the movement within the Churches of Christ was fueled by a desire to teach, train, and develop leaders, they slowly became like many other churches. Ketcherside and Garrett had become prophetic in their warnings to these transitional churches, but these churches followed the way of others in their transition. Ketcherside believed that evangelists had authority that involved elder development and appointment.

In my own experience with Mutual Edification and transitional churches I found that most people were well educated (many times self educated) in the Bible and teaching classes. Men were trained in various aspects of worship and church leadership such as teaching, preaching, song leading, and studying with people about the church. The women were teachers and Bible students who were filled with great acts of charity and love. The evangelists carried a sense of authority and respect (even though they were not paid well). The evangelists constantly identified potential elders and trained these men to lead. They practiced the "Paul and Timothy model" where the evangelist had the authority to oversee the church until elders were appointed. He developed elders because it was biblical, necessary for the church to grow, and enabled him to go on to start and develop another congregation.

This evangelistic oversight was also present in the movement known as the International Churches of Christ. In the late 1970s, the Crossroads Church of Christ in Gainesville, Florida, began to model a very powerful campus ministry and preacher training program.[6] The movement grew, developed many campus ministers, and helped campus ministries in churches grow. Boston, Massachusetts eventually became a major hub for this ministry, which grew into a worldwide missions/church-planting movement within the Churches of Christ. In the late 1980s the "Boston Movement" parted ways with the mainline Churches of Christ. The movement adopted the title International Churches of Christ to reflect their world view of evangelism and the kingdom of God. By the turn of the century, the movement had successfully planted churches in major cities worldwide.

This movement had many strengths, one of which involved the authority carried by the evangelists who practiced evangelistic oversight. Elders were developed in few of the existing congregations and the evangelists led the churches throughout the world. Other evangelists practiced oversight over various "world sectors." "In many cases the evangelist would direct the affairs of the congregation without the elders' and/or lay leadership's serious consultation."[7]

Fortunately, the evangelists continued to focus on outreach and evangelism, but the congregations suffered because they had a deep need for shepherding and spiritual development within the membership. Congregations with a membership of over one thousand had few elders, and due to the rapid growth of the churches they struggled in the spiritual development of their members. In 2002 serious accusations of spiritual abuse and neglect from other leaders led to upheaval and an implosion of congregations and the organization. The movement today has experienced tremendous trauma and is deeply wounded, due to inward tensions between members and leaders.

The movement has few elders to help them through this transition. They have begun to emphasize elder development because they have acknowledged a need for shepherding. Their evangelists and elders have manifested supportive leadership and addressing many of their inward tensions.[8] My personal experience with many of the leaders and members leads me to believe that they are working extremely hard to heal and correct their past issues. An emphasis on elder development will move their churches forward, and I believe that they will continue to heal, return to growth, and continue to proclaim the gospel to the world.

Both the Mutual Edification churches and the International Churches of Christ have experienced a struggle in the roles of elders and evangelists. Both movements have a desire to empower evangelists to reach out into the community. The Mutual Edification congregations suffered because they needed a local evangelist to call them into their communities. The International churches suffered because they needed local shepherds/elders to help them mature. Yet, both movements have challenged the "mainline" churches to address the authority of evangelists.

I acknowledge that evangelists have authority from God (Eph. 4:11-16; 2 Tim. 4:5). I acknowledge that we as preachers have to call the church to growth and outreach. I acknowledge that many times we ministers must shepherd people. But I also acknowledge that many times we are dangerously close to being senior pastors, which God has not called us to be, unless we share the load and keep our focus on outreach. I also acknowledge that we ministers are tired of shepherding and fighting over who is "in charge." As Jethro encouraged Moses to appoint other leaders (Exod. 18:17-23), so we must develop shepherds. God desires community and teamwork in leadership. We need elders to shepherd the church and we must work with them, not under, over, or apart from them, in helping the church to grow and mature. God has called leaders to work as a team and share the leadership responsibilities by using their gifts.

Lord You Keep Him Humble; We'll Keep Him Poor

A second response to this leadership crisis has been to *diminish the influence of the evangelists*. To keep the evangelists from being "too elevated because of their surpassingly great revelations (and training or degree)," they are given elders to torment them, or so we believe. This idea suggests that God provided us with elders to make decisions for the church and keep the evangelists from having too much authority. Elders fulfill the hierarchical role that is needed to "run" the church. This is a response to abuses in leadership, not the scriptures. We have seen church leadership reflect the military (chain of command), government (decisions made behind closed doors), business (board of directors with a preacher/CEO structure), farming (protecting the cattle and delegating the feeding to others), and most recently, the business team dynamics (authority stems from skill/giftedness). Guder suggests that historically church leadership has seen the minister as counselor, manager, and/or technician.[9] All of these have been attempts to define or redefine leadership for the present church. Some have worked; others have not. Some have been of great value for one generation and damaging to the next. Yet, we continue to operate with a hierarchical leadership. While a hierarchy can be helpful in addressing problems or controlling what happens in a church it is not the most efficient method of empowering people to do ministry. It can promote a sense of co-dependency in people.

What have we created? It is hard to speak for all churches, but notice the reaction on a member's face when one says, "One of the elders is coming to visit you this week." I have mentioned involving elders with Christian colleges to pray for the teachers and found a sense of panic from the administration. I know that many congregations have a deep love for preachers and elders and their united leadership. I know that there are elders and ministers who have a close relationship. I know that there are stories of bad elders and bad power-hungry preachers. I know that there are money-hungry preachers, and there are elders who say (about the preacher), "Lord you keep him humble and we'll keep him poor."

So I do not think I am exaggerating when I say that sometimes there seems to be a love-hate relationship between elders and ministers. We have co-existed side by side, but have we acknowledged that we need each other? I find that this is especially true with respect to minister's attitudes toward elders. Do we believe that we need elders? Do we believe that elders are an option/luxury or a necessity for a healthy church?

The problem will only get worse. Each generation since the Builders (those of the WWII generation, born before 1946) has less and less respect for authority. As a Baby Boomer (those born in 1946-1965), I have seen leadership fail, become hypocritical, and turn a deaf ear to those suffering from oppression. I, along with my generation, will not tolerate a poor example from leaders. We are concerned about social justice and feel that the church has ignored (and sometimes enabled our society to continue to practice) major sins such as racism, abuse, economic oppression, and misogyny. The Postmodern generations (the generations following the Baby Boomers to the present) consists of many young people who are quickly losing faith in authority and leadership. They wish to address social justice and engage rather than disengage from our world. "Postmoderns distrust authority and authority structures. They want to see Christ through persons who have earned their respect and trust."[10]

In response to the attitudes of Postmoderns the church has tried to adapt and bring the gospel anew to a generation that distrusts faith communities. Terms such as "Emerging Churches" or "Emergent Churches" have been used to suggest that new churches arise in a culture that is now labeled "Post-Christian." We live in a world that is rejecting Christianity as the guiding voice in their life. They may love God, Jesus, and have a sense of spirituality—yet they do not have the respect (as North America once had) for the church. This presents churches and leaders with a challenge in presenting the gospel.

The Urgency of Training Elders

I suggest that we, along with other ministries, support a third option to meet this need. I believe that *we should train and develop emerging elders for the future*. I believe that we should teach ministers and churches to have an ongoing elder development, training, and selection program. Just as we have trained and developed preachers/ministers, so we should train and develop elders. Emerging leaders are those who arise in times of crisis and spiritual growth. Leaders are those who emerge to gain respect and trust of the congregation. They need to be identified, prepared, and trained for leadership tasks.

Elders should not be appointed and left to find their place in the church. Elders, and other leaders, are not Christians who need to grow—they should already be mature. We do not appoint them so that they might become more active or responsible. Elders should be prepared to lead and serve in a church that believes they are called to fulfill a divine task. I know that most elders work full time and shepherd after hours; therefore I feel that ministers should make elder selection, development, and training a priority in their ministry.

Training elders is an urgent task! Countless elders tell me they were never taught *how* to shepherd. Yet, they know *what* an elder is supposed to be. However, we seem to treat elder selection as an afterthought. Liberal scholars suggest that since Paul thought that Jesus was returning soon he did not initially set up church structure or leadership. They suggest that when he (and the early church) realized that Jesus was not returning in their lifetime, leadership then became an issue. [11] This is why some suggest that Paul was not the author of 1-2 Timothy and Titus is because they have well developed leadership structures.[12] According to this, it seems that church structure was neither part of Jesus' vision nor the mission of the early church. Some scholars also suggest that the Pastoral Epistles were written by someone from the second generation (after Paul) who realized that they needed leadership structure for the church to continue in the future. Evangelism, according to this way of thinking, did not plan for congregational leadership nor did it seek to form congregations that provide structure for future generations. While I believe that these scholars are misinformed, I do feel sometimes that we have validated their claims by our practices. Is church structure necessary for growth and development of the congregation or is it an afterthought?

I believe that we can look to Acts and see the importance of elder development by the way that Paul and Barnabas appointed elders. Paul and Barnabas had finished a section of their first mission trip and decided to return through the Galatian region to appoint elders.

> Then they returned to Lystra, Iconium, and Antioch, strengthening the disciples and encouraging them to remain true to the faith. They told them, "We must go through many hardships to enter the kingdom of God." Paul and Barnabas appointed elders in each church and with prayer and fasting, committed them to the Lord, in whom they had put their trust. (Acts 14:21-23)

Elders in these churches were likely to be fairly recent converts. A study of the timeline of Paul and Barnabas' first missionary journey suggests that those men who were appointed elders in the first congregations had been Christians no more than one and one-half years.[13]

The church in Crete also gives evidence of newer converts as elders. At Crete, being a new convert was not a disqualification for the position of elder.[14] The church at Crete was a new congregation with leaders open to moral criticism (Titus 1:13). For example, Winter suggests that most Cretan men molested their sons as a rite of passage into manhood.[15] The congregation did not have the stability that we see at Ephesus (see 1 and 2 Timothy), and it had temporary evangelists. Titus was sent to quickly appoint elders since he was going to be replaced by Artemas or Tychicus (Titus 3:12). Titus was told to avoid Jewish type discussions (1:14; 3:9-11) and encourage the Cretan Christians to focus on good deeds and moral living (1:13; 2:7, 14; 3:8, 14). It seems that the congregation had a stronger Gentile presence. Paul's ministry was also heavily focused on God-fearers and Gentiles.[16] Any man appointed as an elder would have been Gentile and a Christian for only a short time.

There have been many suggestions as to why Paul and Barnabas appointed new converts in the Gentile congregations. The most common argument is that Paul *may have* appointed Jewish men or proselytes as elders.[17] These men would have known the *Torah* (Jewish law of Moses) and the ways of *Yahweh* (the Hebrew name of God). While this is a good argument, it is one based on silence. The text doesn't tell us this. I think it is also based on an unwillingness to admit that Paul appointed newer converts in *some churches*.

Paul appointed newer Gentile converts as elders in *some churches*, most likely the newer church plants. First, I think that the silence of the text leaves the possibility open for the acceptance of Gentile elders. Second, we must remember that it was the Jewish view of the law that caused problems in many of Paul's congregations, not the Gentile's ignorance concerning the law. In the early congregations Paul told the Christians to hold to his teachings and then proceeded to discuss the true understanding of the law (Rom. 3; Gal. 1:6-9; 2 Thess. 2:15). Third, many of Paul's churches began in cities without a strong Jewish presence. Luke told us that there was a synagogue at Psidian Antioch and at Iconium but we do not see a strong Jewish community at Lystra, Derbe, or Crete. Paul and Barnabas would not have many (if any) Jewish men to choose as elders. It is also interesting that Paul's pattern of church planting was to leave an evangelist behind to appoint leaders (Titus 1:3-6). In Acts, Luke does not mention that Paul addressed the synagogue in Philippi and Athens, which suggests a minimal Jewish presence. Leadership, in many of these cities, would have had to come from Gentile converts. Fourth, in Romans 14 Paul suggested that the Jewish Christians were the "weak ones" in the faith. Would leadership come exclusively from this group? Fifth, the Greek term *neophyte* is defined as a recently baptized person, not one who has been a Christian less than a few years. Finally, since Paul was combating the circumcision party in Psidian Antioch and Iconium (Acts 13-14) it is likely that he would have tried to create a mix in leadership. This mix would effectively lead both Jew and Gentile Christians. If the church were predominantly Gentile it would be likely that Paul would appoint Gentiles as elders.

It is reasonable to suggest, therefore, that Paul and Barnabas *appointed* as elders Gentile Christians who had been in the faith for one to two years. While Paul restricted newly baptized men (*neophytes*) from leading as elders at Ephesus (1 Tim. 3:6), for some reason he did not place this restriction on elders at Crete or some of the cities in Syria.

I am not, however, suggesting that we appoint new converts to be leaders. We do need to understand that a new convert is one who is less than a year old as a Christian. The work of shepherding is a heavy load, and elders are thrown into great temptation. I am suggesting that elder development be one of the major ministries we begin with a new congregation. I am suggesting that missionaries immediately seek out husbands and wives who are strong and able to develop shepherding skills. I am suggesting that elder development and evangelism go together. I am suggesting that we train ministers and missionaries to identify and develop husband/wife couples to become shepherds so that the evangelists can focus on outreach rather than shepherding.

One of the issues we should address in elder development is the role of an elder's wife. Deacon's wives have a role (1 Tim. 3:11) and some apostles/preachers were accompanied in their ministry by their wives (1 Cor. 9:5). Because of this, an elder's wife is more than a qualification. She can become an active partner and play a vibrant role in working with her husband as a team to support and shepherd the women of the church. Paul encourages Titus to have older women (Titus 2:3-5) play an active role in helping younger women mature spiritually. Elders' wives can fulfill this role of leadership in the church by working with women. Elders' wives can also help their husbands promote a less intimidating atmosphere in which to work with women who struggle with sin or have issues specific to females which men may not understand.

In my elder development project at the Metro Church of Christ, the elders' wives had developed a wonderful ministry for the women of the congregation, including singles, divorced, young parents, older women, and others. They took responses from women after the sermon (commonly called the invitation) and developed a strong bond with many of the women in the church. This, in my opinion, is a ministry that many churches have neglected.

Churches need elders. God wants churches to have elders. Elders empower preachers and ministers to focus on evangelism and outreach. Elders are needed to help the members grow, develop, and mature in the faith. If elders are needed, then we need to institute development programs for these Christians. We need to have ongoing training to identify and strengthen men and their wives who can shepherd churches so that they can grow, thrive, and mature in their communities and the world.

Questions

1. What is the connection between church growth and the role of the preacher?

2. How has elder development been used in the Restoration Movement, past and present?

3. How have we diminished the influence/authority of the evangelist?

4. Has elder development been a priority in your experience? Why or why not?

5. Paul and Barnabas appointed Christians as elders who were likely less than two years old spiritually? Do you agree with this interpretation? Why or why not? How does your church's interpretation impact our selection of elders today?

Chapter 2

SHEPHERDS AND GROWING FLOCKS

"Pastors have given themselves to ministering only to the pain of their congregations but have failed to mobilize their congregations to minister to the pain and problems of the city. Either we learn to do both or reaching our cities for Christ will be nothing more than a hope and dream."[18]

When elders and their wives actively shepherd in their congregations, the preachers will be able to focus more on outreach and evangelism. We, like many other church movements, are not growing. While there have been many efforts for unity and reconciliation among the Christian Churches, Churches of Christ, and International Churches, I believe that this will not solve our lack of growth in America. Our movement faces a future that is filled with tension, a need for healing, and a constant challenge to continue to focus on preaching Jesus to a changing world and our communities. The United States is quickly becoming one of the most unchurched countries in the world. Notice the following statistics:

- Previously 4,000 churches in America closed each year while less than 1,500 opened.[19] In 2006, however, for the first time in decades—more churches were started in America than were closed.[20] This new statis-

tic was done among conservative Evangelical churches. Church planting in the Restoration Movement has most effectively been done by the
International churches and Christian Churches, while the Churches of
Christ have not been able to keep pace with others. It is safe to say that we
still continue to face a growth crisis in the Restoration Movement.

- U.S. churches are losing at least 3 million people a year to nonreligious
  lifestyles.[21]
- Fifty percent of U.S. churches did not record one conversion the previous
  year.[22]
- In 1965, thirty-nine percent of the U.S. was unchurched; in 2004, sixty-
  one percent was unchurched (unchurched is defined as having attended
  0 or 1 times in the past year).[23] However, the Barna group estimates that
  in 2004 this statistic was only thirty-five percent. Various other groups
  report higher statistics but the consensus among church growth prac-
  titioners is that the statistics are lower, some as low as fifteen percent.
  However one reads the statistics it is clear that the church is not growing
  in North America.
- Sixty-two percent of America's 400,000 Protestant churches are declining
  in membership.[24]
- Eighty-four percent of American churches are growing at a slower rate
  than their community's growth rate, which is twenty-one percent per
  year.[25]
- Only twenty-nine percent (three out of ten) new members are assimi-
  lated (kept) in a church over a five year period.[26]
- Today's church is losing its grip on the very world it has been called to
  save.[27]
- The Churches of Christ have experienced almost no numerical growth in
  the United States from 1980 to 2000.[28]

It is clear from the se statistics that growth is minimal in American
churches. In spite of all the work that has been done by the Evangelical churches
concerning evangelism, churches still struggle to grow. "Even though some $500

billion has been spent on church growth materials and seminars during the last fifteen years, the percentage of evangelicals in this country is actually smaller now than before."[29] Preachers and elders in Restoration Movement churches can function as a unit and together focus on evangelism. Preachers cannot carry this responsibility alone—especially if the elders feel that they do not have a responsibility to set an example in supporting outreach.

- "Only one out of three pastors—*pastors*—believes the church is making a positive impact on the culture."[30]
- Growing churches have pastors who believe in the Great Commission.[31]
- Pastors need to adapt their leadership styles to the size and growth of the congregation.[32]

These statistics suggest that the preachers/pastors have a tremendous effect on the direction of the church. But, if the churches are declining, is the blame solely on the preachers? It would seem that this is true. Research on churches over the last quarter century has consistently revealed that one of the central differences between growing churches and declining churches is a pastor who believes God wants his church to grow."[33] As a preacher, I find that most ministers have a conviction for the Great Commission. I also find that most ministers are frustrated rather than apathetic about church growth. Why?

One possibility is that ministers are overworked and overburdened with the responsibilities of shepherding. Church growth books have suggested that we need to delegate or distribute the work to other members and "lay leaders." Terms such as "ranching," "purpose driven," "highly effective," and others are commonly used at conferences designed to teach ministers how to involve their members in evangelism. An important office that God has ordained for the church is being neglected. Elders are appointed to help the evangelists keep their focus on outreach. This only works if we have an effective model of church leadership that encourages leaders to pursue their giftedness.

Another possibility is that *preachers are promoting a clergy/laity system.* Rather than encouraging elders to model evangelism and the church to join them in the work, preachers make a distinction between the evangelizer and the member. "Ministers alone may administer the sacraments or, as a rule, preach the Word. Ruling elders, but only in the same way as other men, may preach, if licensed by a presbytery to do so."[34] This is an example in the Presbyterian churches where a distinction is made between preaching and shepherding. In John 4:1 Jesus' disciples baptized other people. Ministers must empower others, as Jesus did, to evangelize, baptize, and disciple people.

Third, *some ministers do not become involved in their communities.* I understand that every minister is gifted in different ways. Some are scholars, some not. Some are people oriented and extroverted; others are introverts. I know that some ministers struggle with organization and others struggle with accepting disorder in their schedules. However, if a church wants to reach the lost they do need to call their minister to set the pace for them. Elders need to be clear concerning what the church needs from their ministers, and elders need to develop ways of shepherding ministers to keep their focus on the vision of Christ for the congregation. Ministers also need to be aware if their gifts are more pastoral, if they are more valuable as hospice chaplains, or if they are evangelists. Too often we have gifted ministers serving in the wrong churches. It is important to match the gift and ministry with the right church.

Finally, the decline *may be an indication that churches are not developing a heart for the lost.* Sermons call us to evangelism, but we easily convince ourselves that staff can be evangelistic because they are paid to do so. It is easy to assume that it is someone else's responsibility. This results in a sense of apathy and a withdrawal from the community.

Why are churches experiencing minimal growth? Is it possible that preachers have become pastors and the members have become sheep with an overworked or inattentive shepherd? Schools train ministers to do pastoral work, at the expense of church growth. I traveled to Toluca, Mexico (with two elders and one of their wives) to conduct a training session on elder development. The church had a preacher training school in their building. After the training the director asked, "Why aren't we incorporating this in our preacher/minister trainings?" I responded, "I don't know, but I can tell you that this is also missing in many of our university ministry courses."

Elders can help churches grow and become healthy and more effective. First, *elders can shepherd the flock and attend to their needs*. Elders can model for the congregation a spiritual life and desire for outreach. They can support the preacher by encouraging and reaching out to the lost while shepherding the church. They can set an example to the church not only in morals but also in evangelism.

Second, *elders can remove some of the emotional stress from the ministers and encourage them to keep focused on outreach*. Ministers struggle in many areas because they are on the front lines of the community, calling the lost to Jesus. They need to be shepherded and guided while they practice a ministry that demands risk and faith. If elders assume the task of shepherding, preachers can focus on outreach. Instead of competing, ministers and elders can *support each other and work together* to develop the congregation. Elders acting as pastors can help a church become more effective because all leaders then can use their giftedness.

How Are Elders Valuable in Spiritual Growth?

The position of elder is an important one that has been ordained by God. The early church appointed elders, and Jesus gave elders as a gift to the congregation because they were important for the growth and outreach of the church (Eph. 4:7-11). Jesus believed that churches needed pastors and preachers, as well as other leadership offices. God believes that churches can mature and develop when the role of shepherds is distinct from the role of preachers/ministers. Why should we train and develop elders? God wants churches to have overseers. God obviously believes that churches with these leaders have a better chance to grow and reach the world for Jesus. Elders have always provided a key role in the health and growth of God's people.

Who are Elders?

In the ancient Near East, elders were men who worked with the heads of clans to help govern the nomadic and early tribal states. They were important in the life and growth of the tribe. As the civilizations transitioned to a centralized head/leader, the elders' influence diminished (as seen in the time of the Judges). The judge/savior took the responsibility to lead the people, and the power/authority of the elders decreased. After the time of the Judges but still in pre-monarchy era, the elders' responsibilities once again grew. Elders began to expand their authority to help other leaders and the people of Israel.

> During the pre-monarchic period, the Israelite elders, as heads of set-
> tlements and family units, enjoyed wide-ranging authority to a greater
> extent than those in other countries in the Ancient Near East whose
> power was limited by the royal and state frameworks.[35]

During the time of the kings, the elders again lost their influence. They later gained this authority during the fall of Jerusalem, when there was no Israelite king. When the people returned to Jerusalem the nation began to depend on the leadership of elders, priests, and heads of clans.

During the days of the Dead Sea Scrolls community (Qumran), elders began to work with an overseer called a *mbqr* (1QS 6:8-9; CD 14). This overseer was thirty to fifty-five years old and was responsible for the following:[36]

1. Instructing the community in ways of God.
2. Looking after the mental and physical well-being of the hurting.
3. Examining and classifying new candidates for membership in the community.
4. Protecting the community from outside influences.

Until the time of Jesus, elders provided guidance through monarchy, captivity, and restoration. They provided leadership by living among the people and guiding them in times of crisis.

By the time of Jesus and the New Testament, the elders had become scholars and, for those who lived near Jerusalem, members of the Sanhedrin. Some carried tremendous political power in Jerusalem and were known for defending the faith. They oversaw the synagogues and made sure that the community was protected, preserved, and spiritually developed. Their power came from their communities and from earning the respect of the people.

An elder was ascribed authority by the people of his community who deemed him worthy of respect and honor . . . "The elders were a collective group whose authority was based on the recognition of the people below them."[37] We also know that the political power of the elders of Judah was reflected in the so-called "people of the land," which was influenced by the decisions the elders made.[38] Local elders also worked for reconciliation motivated by reconciliation of a social rift, motivated by moral integrity of their community and social/economic solidarity of their community.[39]

The development of elders historically suggests that they were an office rather than a representative of an age group. They had the best interest of the people in mind. They were in a position to influence the congregation spiritually and emotionally. They showed flexibility in their decision making policies. Finally, they were members of the community and were economically the same status as the congregation.

Elder was an office in the community. Elders were not meant to rule the people; they were meant to work with other leaders to lead people closer to God and to represent their needs. This office is important in that elders live and move among the people to help them grow and develop spiritually. Elders are necessary for the church to grow and for the preacher to continue to focus on outreach and evangelism. Elders reflect the incarnation because they are among the people, with the people, and one of the people. As we discuss incarnational leadership, we will address this more.

How Do Elders Lead?

Elders derive their authority in two ways. First, *they receive authority from their community*. Since they are among the people and lead by example, they are given authority by the respect of their community. This means that elders are respected, honored, and supported by their congregation because they have proven themselves to be leaders. They are given permission to lead, not because of their position but because of their character.

Second, Christian *elders have authority from God and the Holy Spirit* (Acts 20:28). Paul told the elders from Ephesus that the Holy Spirit had made them bishops. This is a key distinction from other elders: Christian shepherds have divine authority.

Elders, I believe, must have both aspects of authority. If they do not have the respect of the people, they are elders in title only. Elders always received authority from the people because they live in their communities and lead by their example. God has not given authority to elders who are not respected by their faith community and secular community. God requires that they have this respect from outsiders, family, and the church. This means that an elder who expects respect from the church simply because he is an elder does not understand incarnational leadership. In Ezekiel 34 God took away the authority of leaders who neither respected the flock nor gained respect from the flock. Elders must have the respect of the church or they cannot lead.

It is easy to say, "I have authority from God, therefore . . ." Some preachers/pastors have demanded respect from people by claiming to have a divine "calling" or "appointment." These ministers often resist accountability, viewing leadership as an office. They do not believe that God works through the people who daily trust and serve them. They do not believe that those who cry out against them may be the voice of God.

The prophets were incarnational. They lived among the people and confronted leaders from the eyes of the masses. The Spirit moved them to speak for God and to represent the suffering of the poor, orphans, widows, and outsiders. Jesus, a common Jew (from the human perspective) who worked among the oppressed, also confronted these leaders who claimed to have a divine calling or appointment. What did he confront them about? He confronted them about violating human rights, oppressing the poor, widows, and aged parents; and thinking that they were "above the law." Nicodemus was a Jewish leader who listened to Jesus and tried to discern the truth. His coming to Jesus at night (John 3:1-2) indicates that he was humble enough to listen to this "prophet." His willingness to question the other Jewish leaders (John 7:51) illustrates his understanding of God's law and people. His presence at the burial of Jesus (John 19:39) hints to us that he was a man who was open to changing his mind.

Incarnational leadership is not about being swayed by popular opinion. It is not about listening to every whim and complaint and taking these personally. It is about listening to, respecting, and being an example to those we serve. We listen because people need to be validated. We hear because people need a voice. We reflect and discern because many times God speaks through the common person, little one, or still small voice. An elder who hears the voice of the flock has a flock that knows his voice (John 10). He receives authority from the people and therefore can receive God's appointment as a leader and shepherd of the congregation.

Conclusion

The position of elder historically existed in the ancient world as well as the world of ancient Israel. Elders are necessary for congregations to grow and develop spiritually. Elders live among the people, and they lead and gain authority by their influence. They also have authority from God to lead those who willingly wish to follow them. While a hierarchy of leadership was common to Israel, leaders empowered and guided the people. Elders also were team players who work with other leaders to protect, help, and develop their communities. Elders today have the opportunity to serve in this ancient office and guide the modern church to health and wholeness. In the next section we will discuss the character and nature of elders.

Questions

1. What is the dilemma facing American churches today?

2. How can the Restoration Movement better address this dilemma?

3. The biblical elder's authority stems from what?

4. How is incarnational leadership practiced by elders?

5. How can elders help the church become more evangelistic?

SECTION TWO

GOOD SHEPHERDS

Chapter 3

THE LORD IS MY SHEPHERD: HOW GOD MODELS LEADERSHIP

If we are paying careful attention to a scriptural understanding of leadership we can't ignore the implied criticism that today's church needs . . . something other than what we are usually offered in contemporary leadership studies. There is a pervasive powerlessness and shrinkage of the church in the West. The leadership lessons from the world have not improved our market share, and the sell out to pragmatism, the heresy of valuing whatever works, has not worked. The kingdom we are building is essentially different from Wal-Mart and the Mormon Church. To the extent that our leadership practices reflect the ways of the world, if we evaluate them fairly, they haven't worked.

Each week fifty-three thousand Christians leave the church in the West, and the United States is now the fifth most unchurched nation on the planet . . . A new generation of Spirit-empowered leaders is needed—right here, right now.[40]

The Bible teaches that God is both bishop and pastor. God's desire is to transform lives and prepare people for ministry. God leads people with a view to their security and encouragement. Jesus imitated God's leadership incarnationally. God also calls other men to bishop and pastor the people by imitating and reflecting the Father's compassion, concern, and love for them. This work could be called *incarnational leadership*.

Shawchuck and Heuser say a church needs four great things: mission, organization, relationships, spirituality.[41]

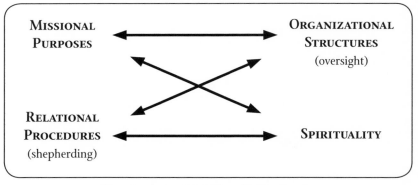

Figure 1—Systems Model For a Healthy Church.

In order to grow spiritually and numerically in the surrounding community, the church needs a leadership development program that trains its elders to lead organizationally and relationally. They help to nurture and strengthen the body of Christ. These methods of leadership are a reflection of God's leadership and are manifestations of God's desire to guide and love the people, including those inside and outside the covenant. God exhibited them in both ancient Israel and the first century church. Jesus modeled God's leadership style through the incarnation. Church leaders also model God's leadership incarnationally.[42] These leaders are appointed to imitate God's care and concern for people. God uses church leaders and the congregation to transform individuals who in turn transform their culture and society.[43]

God Leads People by Giving Attention to Them

God's Oversight

First, God led people organizationally by being attentive. God was a bishop to the people. In the Hebrew scriptures, oversight can be understood by the use of the terms *paqad*, *baqar*, *r'ah*, *tsadeq*, and *mishpat*. These Hebrew terms involved seeing, appointing, and practicing justice and righteousness. God knew the people and appointed leadership in order to guide, protect, or deliver the children. The most common term used for God's concern is *pqd*. This term meant "attend to,"[44] "appoint,"[45] "visit,"[46] or "oversee."[47] The Akkadian (an ancient language before Hebrew) equivalent of this word meant to supervise, appoint, or put in charge.[48] *Pqd* was also used for a governor or other high-ranking official. It indicated leadership that involved delegation. While it may suggest, to the modern reader, a sense of power and control, in the ancient world it suggested an individual who cared for others. Chaos and disorder were characteristics of evil. Organization and order were characteristics of good. God, who controls chaos, gave attention to and came to the aid of Israel (Gen. 50:24, 25; Ex. 13:19), watched over the nation (Ex. 3:16; Job 10:12; 29:4), was concerned for them (Ex. 4:31), and took a seat in heaven to see the earth (Ps. 109:8). God was actively involved with people and "looked after" the group in order to address their needs.

The term *pqd* also referred to judgment. God's visitation sometimes involved judgment, punishment, or vindication (Is. 10:3; Jer. 6:15; 10:15; 11:23; 24:22; 29:6). When God visited the people, they were saved because their enemies were judged or disciplined. *Pqd* indicated that God was always ready to respond on behalf of Israel's actions and needs.

Yahweh was the king who also commanded others to work and guide Israel. In the Greek text of the Old Testament, *pqd* was most often translated *episkopos*.[49] This Greek term is the same word used for bishop or overseer in the New Testament (Acts 20:28; 1 Tim. 3:8; 1 Peter 5:2).[50] God visited the people (Luke 19:44; 1 Peter 2:12), and Jesus oversaw the condition of his church (1 Peter 2:25). Early church writers such as Ignatius and Clement also believed that God gave attention to the congregation and kingdom.[51]

Oversight was a term used to describe God's leadership of the nation. God watched, appointed leaders, and visited the people. God was the king who looked to the needs of people and sent help, organizationally, for them. God practiced oversight and responded to their cries. Organizational leadership involved oversight, appointment, and giving attention to the needs of the group. Due to the nature of the Emerging Church culture a newer definition should be stressed. While the older definition "oversight" did not give the full meaning of God's leadership I am using the term "give attention to." Why should elders be concerned about "giving attention" to their congregations?

- Child neglect is damaging to children and becoming a common issue with those living in our world. Neglect has been found to be more dangerous to the emotional development of people than abuse. People who have been neglected need to know that God gives attention to their needs.
- Many young people feel that church leaders (as well as political and business leaders) do not hear their voices or opinions.
- Leadership has traditionally neglected the needs of others. This is not God's nature.
- This is a challenge for future leaders to give attention in their ministry to others.

God's leadership was also defined by the Hebrew term *r'ah*. This term is translated "to see," and it expressed God's response while overseeing the people.[52] God looked upon the status of Sarah (Gen. 21:1); saw the danger for Isaac, the land, and the congregation (Gen. 22:8, 14[53]; Deut. 11:12; Zeph. 2:7); came to the aid of the people (Ruth 1:6); and watched from heaven (Ps. 80:14). The act of seeing indicated that *Yahweh* had a concern for the nation and cared for them. The overseer paid attention to people and was aware of their needs.

God also responded as an overseer by hearing the cries of the people. In Judges, the nation cried to God, who responded (Judg. 3:9, 15; 6:8; 10:16). Moses was told that God had already seen (*r'ah*) and heard the cry of the Israelites and was responding to them (Ex. 3:7).[54] God saw the suffering and listened to the cries of the people. When they cried out, God responded (Is. 65:24; Dan. 9:19).

God saw, heard, and responded to the needs of people. God established the creation (Gen. 1; Ps. 8) and also appointed deliverers and servants (Judg. 3:9, 15; Is. 42:1-4). God came to their rescue through delegation and punitive deliverance. God sent national saviors and foreign kings to deliver and judge enemies from other nations (Is. 45:1-4). When the people sinned and rebelled, God saw and then appointed other rulers and nations to punish them. God, who is righteous (*tsadeq*) and just (*mishpat*), also responded to the cry of the poor and weak.[55] *Yahweh* continued to hear the cry of the oppressed and afflicted and vindicated them (Prov. 21:13; 22:22-23; 23:10-11).

God's Care and Concern

God's care is also illustrated by the word *bqr*.[56] This is seen in the development of the word *bqr* during the Persian period (also *episkopos* in the Greek version of the Old Testament). This word was used in both Hebrew and Aramaic for inspector, overseer, caregiver, or administrator. Ezra was sent by the Persian Empire to be an administrator over the territories that were being rebuilt. He came to search (Ezra 6:2), visit or oversee (7:14), and give attention to the needs of the people (4:15, 19). The *mbqr* was also an official at Qumran (the location of the community that wrote and preserved the Dead Sea Scrolls) who served as the administrator of the community. His responsibility was to teach the law, examine the initiates, act as guardian of the community, and handle the finances of the group (1QS 6:11-12, 19-20; CD 9:18-19; 13:13; 15:11, 14). He gave attention to the community to protect and develop them.

> He shall love them as a father loves his children, and shall carry them in all their distress like a shepherd his sheep. He shall loosen all the fetters which bind them that in his Congregation there may be none that are oppressed or broken. He shall examine every man entering his Congregation with regard to his deeds, understanding, strength, ability, and possessions, and shall inscribe him in his place according to his rank . . . no member of the camp shall have authority to admit a man to the Congregation against the decision of the Guardian (*mbqr*) of the camp (CD 13:8-14).

The Hebrew term *mbqr* and Greek term *episkopos* carry both organizational and relational meanings and suggest that a bishop/elder is involved with people.

Caring Incarnationally

Christ modeled God's leadership style by showing concern for and awareness of the sinfulness of God's people. God appointed Jesus to provide care and concern for people. Peter wrote that Jesus is the "overseer of our souls" (*episko-pos*, 1 Peter 2:25). To oversee meant to show concern and care for people or one's affairs. Jesus saw and heard the suffering cries of his people and responded with salvation and healing. Jesus practiced his Father's organizational leader-ship incarnationally through attention and care.[57]

Leadership in the Bible involved imitating God's concern and appoint-ing helpers. *Pqd* and *episkopos* were terms used for leaders who gave attention to the various work and military activities of the nation. Leaders counted (Ex. 30:12) took charge of troops or work details (Num. 4:16; 7:2; 31:14; 2 Kings 11:15, 18; 12:11; Ezra 4:15, 19; 7:14; Neh. 11:9, 14, 22; 2 Chron. 34:12, 17) or took stock of property (Job. 5:24). These leaders also practiced organizational leadership by looking after others (Ezra 6:1, 7:15; Esther 2:11).

The early church practiced this leadership by looking after (*episkopos*) others who were struggling relationally in the body of Christ (Heb. 12:15). *Episkopon* was most commonly used for elders who were to give attention to the needs of the congregation. Bishops were to practice organizational lead-ership through awareness of and attentiveness to the needs of the saints. Paul encouraged the elders to "watch out for the flock," and Peter encouraged them to "give attention to the flock" (Acts 20:25; 1 Peter 5:2-4).

A theological task for modern leaders is to practice incarnational leadership through attention and concern for people. This ministry is not about control or "lording it over the flock" but about attending to the needs of the congregation (1 Peter 5:3). It is about awareness. It involves per-sonal investment. Elders must be concerned with the condition and needs of a congregation. To practice *episkopos* or *pqd* means to see and apply the necessary resources to guide a congregation to spiritual health. Leaders who give attention approach congregational issues with vision, concern, and awareness. They appoint, delegate, oversee, and attend to the health of the church and each member. "The authority of overseers is not dependent upon whether people judge them to be good men but it is whether or not people are willing to participate with them, according to James and Evelyn Whitehead."[58]

God Leads People Through Relational Leadership

God Shepherds People Relationally

Another style of God's leadership is relational. God existed in a relationship with people and led them throughout time. God's relationship was manifested most commonly through covenant. God was always the initiator of the covenant. Covenant was established because *Yahweh* loved the people and chose to establish and maintain this relationship through faithfulness and love (Deut. 7:4-11). Covenant was begun, maintained, and re-established through *Yahweh's* compassion, mercy, and love. "God's disclosure of himself is not grasped speculatively, not expounded in the form of a lesson; it is as [if] he breaks in on the life of his people in his dealings with them and moulds them according to his will that he grants them knowledge of his being."[59] God's covenant was conditional; faithfulness and loyalty by people was expected. God's love was unconditional; however, God was always willing to restore the sinful nation to a relationship.[60]

> The use of the covenant concept in secular life argues that the religious *berit* [Hebrew for covenant] too was always regarded as a bilateral relationship; for even though the burden's most unequally distributed between the two contracting parties, this makes no difference to the fact that the relationship is still essentially two sided.

> With this God men know exactly where they stand; an atmosphere of trust and security is created, in which they find both the strength for a willing surrender to the will of God and joyful courage to grapple with the problems of life.[61]

The relational aspect of leadership was expressed in Ps. 78:52-53.

> God brought the people out like a flock; and led them like sheep through the desert. God guided them safely, so they were not afraid; but the sea engulfed their enemies.[62]

Yahweh led the people into the wilderness and guided them with love and compassion so that they would not fear any danger. Psalm 23 described *Yahweh* as a shepherd who also guided the sheep in love. *Yahweh* condemned the Israelite shepherds who failed to lead with this type of compassion (Ezek. 34:1-11; Jer. 23:1-4). *Yahweh*, as shepherd, leads with compassion, love, and faithfulness.[63]

Incarnational Shepherding

Jesus also practiced God's relational form of leadership. In John 10 he claimed to be the good shepherd who gave his life for the sheep. The Father gave this relational authority as a shepherd to Jesus (10:18). Jesus reflected his Father's leadership style as a faithful shepherd (10:11). His death was an indication that he was giving in his relationships with others. In Acts 20:28 Paul stated that Jesus purchased the church, as a shepherd, with his blood. Peter also wrote that Jesus was the "chief shepherd," who called the elders to account for the sheep. "When the chief shepherd appears, you will receive an unfading crown of glory" (1 Peter 5:4).

Jesus' love and compassion was a reflection of his Father's leadership style. He embodied both caring and relationship with people.

Christian leaders, bearing God's own image, are to lead relationally. While organization is necessary in leadership, it is only part of God's leadership style. God expects elders to show compassion, faithfulness, and love in leadership. Shepherds know and care for their sheep. People will not follow leaders unless there is a relationship. In the Bible, human leaders were called shepherds (Is. 56:11; Jer. 10:21; 50:44; 1 Chron. 11:2). In Ezekiel 34 the term referred to Israelite leaders. The leaders were to shepherd as *Yahweh* had shepherded. Their abuse of power angered God, who promised to replace them with David or the Messianic Shepherd (Ezek. 34:23). Jesus, as the Good Shepherd, gave his life for the sheep and modeled God's style of leadership (John 10:1-18). Elders were commanded to shepherd and lead the flock through oversight (Acts 20:28) and as willing examples (1 Peter 5:4). The early church expected its leaders to reflect God and Christ by serving and leading relationally.

Leaders reflect God's leadership model and imitate Christ by guiding the people. God modeled a leadership style over the flock that was both organizational and relational. God did this through care, concern, giving attention, and relationship. It is the responsibility of elders to develop relationships and show attention to God's people. They must reflect God's compassion, mercy, delegation, and attentiveness as they lead the flock. In order to shepherd God's flock, the elders need to be personally involved in the lives of God's children.

Since incarnational leadership involves practicing God's and Christ's leadership style, it is important to apply this style to a modern context. How do elders oversee and shepherd people? What is involved in attending to, sharing within a covenant, and guiding the congregation? How do mere men, as elders, imitate a divine, all-powerful, benevolent, and merciful God among their fellow brothers and sisters in Christ? A working model is needed for elders to imitate God's method of leadership.

Elders need to model their ministry after the pattern that God has set through the scriptures and in Christ. In a changing world, the tasks of visitation, concern, and attention are demanding. The elders need to find a way to model God's styles of ministry to the congregation. Elders can be relational by practicing compassion and encouraging faithfulness to God and the community of faith.

GOD'S LEADERSHIP IN A MODERN CONTEXT: OVERSIGHT AND SHEPHERDING

Historical/Traditional Leadership

I am a convert to Christianity and not familiar with many of the past leadership styles in churches. My experience in the church has been regional (Midwest) but I understand that leadership in those churches is similar to that throughout the country. From research on the "mutual ministry" congregations in the Churches of Christ, I have found that their leadership practices are very different from those of congregations with full-time, paid, local preachers.

The literature written about "mainline congregations" indicates that the elders had a tendency to act as a board of directors and operate with a hierarchical form of leadership. In this style of leadership, the elders follow a "top down" method of leading. They were selected by the congregation to make decisions and were more concerned with control than delegation.[64] This is a characteristic of the "Builder" (Pre-World War II) generation, which trusted and supported leadership even if it failed to gain the full respect of people. Since the 1960s, however, our generations and culture do not give such respect easily to leaders. Leadership must earn that respect. Whether we like it or not, this is how people are today. Leadership is greatly valued when it earns respect. Current generations also will stand with leadership and become loyal when they are convinced that leaders are genuine.

It is interesting to me that the mutual ministry congregations started out with elders who trained and developed other members, but through time they also developed a board of directors mentality. Through my interviews with these congregations, I found that as the congregations began to decline, the evangelists became more concerned with holding to the mutual ministry pattern and took on more of an evangelistic oversight role in order to keep the congregations together.[65] I believe that elders desire to bishop and shepherd biblically, but the influences of tradition and culture and the demands of larger congregations make it difficult for them to redefine their leadership roles. This book seeks to encourage them to search the Scriptures, imitate God's style of leadership in Christ (incarnational leadership), and plow new ground for the role of elders.

Business leader models have been highly influential in church leadership, especially during the 1980s and 1990s. While this has heavily influenced church leadership, I think that the model is not based on God's style of leadership but on what people desire from their leaders. This model works from the bottom up. While I acknowledge that our view of spiritual issues many times is seen in the lives of Christians; I think that it is always better to begin at the top. Our source of leadership and vision should be theological rather than anthropological.[66]

Dodd, quoted at the beginning of this chapter, has hit us with a tremendous challenge. Either we let the business world determine how to lead our churches and develop leaders, or we let God show us. I acknowledge that some of the principles are good, but shouldn't we begin with God? What does God require of leaders? What does God say about leadership? How does God lead people? How do elders model God's leadership? Most importantly, who should we appoint that will model God's style of leadership?

In figure 3, God's leadership is reflected to the church through Christ and church leaders. This leadership is then manifested to the world.

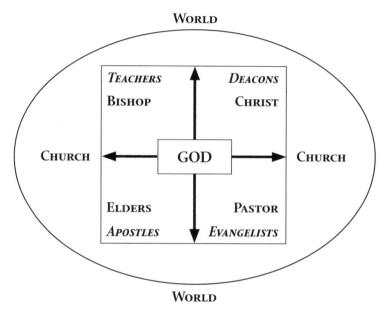

Figure 2—God's Leadership Reflected through Christ, Leaders, and the Church.

God leads the church and world through spiritual attention and shepherding. The elders are to reflect this style of leadership for the church, which in turn reflects leadership for the lost world. Elders can become aware of the condition of God's people (Prov. 27:23).[67]

> Know well the face of your flocks and give attention to your herds. Riches do not endure forever and a crown is not secure for all generations. When the hay is removed and new growth appears, and the grass from the hills is gathered, the lambs will provide you with clothing and the goats with the price of a field. You will have plenty of goats' milk to feed you and your family and to nourish your servant girls.

While they may not take care of each individual themselves they are able to appoint helpers to provide for those Christians struggling with sin, immaturity, and spiritual issues. They do this through 1) prayer, 2) visitation, 3) hospitality, and 4) communication.[68] Elders are also pastors/shepherds. They have a relationship with the flock and practice 1) mercy, 2) compassion, 3) love, 4) forgiveness, and 5) reconciliation in the church. Elders imitate God both organizationally and relationally.

When we talk about biblical leaders, we are talking about those who model God and Christ in the church. Because they follow God, they care about the church, look to the needs of the church, call Christians to accountability and peace, practice mercy and compassion, and develop the spirituality of others. They are men who desire to imitate God, Jesus, and the Spirit. They lead as God leads. They love as Jesus loves. They help develop others spiritually as the Spirit guides and transforms.

In the past I have encouraged congregations to appoint men as elders who would set the direction and lead a church forward. The pressure was on these men to persuade others to follow in their direction. Actually, this is not the model that God has set. God sets the direction. God gives us the plan. God tells the church where it is going. Preachers call the congregation to a vision and work with elders and others to develop the members. Elders nurture all members of the body and at times those in their communities. They have been following God because they are being transformed by the Spirit. They model submission and service. They model obedience. They model the life that God calls all Christians to live. Elders do not have a different standard of life—they prove that they can live by the standard that God has set for all Christians.

Elders also work with other leaders, such as gifted teachers, evangelists, missionaries, deacons, and others. Elders are not called to establish a hierarchy. They are called to empower the church to reach its potential in God's purpose. They shepherd other leaders so that they can develop and lead in their ministries. Elders are called to guide and develop members to be the best that they can be. They are called to bind and heal the weak so that they can go back into battle with Satan. They are called to protect the sick and stray sheep and lead them back to God. They are called to model the ministry of God and Jesus as good shepherds.

GOOD SHEPHERDS MODEL GOD'S STYLE OF LEADERSHIP ORGANIZATIONAL LEADERSHIP

First, oversight/concern means that the elders will need to see and attend to the needs of the flock. Rather than imitate a form of leadership that models power and control, the elders will need to reflect God's organizational style by empowering the flock to grow. Accountability, awareness, visitation, and concern can be used to accomplish this style of oversight.

Accountability

Accountability is one method of oversight and attention. God held the shepherds accountable for their actions (Ezek. 34:10). Jesus, as the chief shepherd, will hold elders accountable for the flock of God (1 Peter 5:4). Accountability means that elders understand their responsibility to reflect God's oversight and attention to the congregation. It also means that they take their duties seriously. The Hebrew writer refers to this as "giving account" to God (Heb. 13:17). Their leadership is to be a positive experience, so that the sheep are persuaded by them and follow their lead (Heb. 13:18).[69] Elders must persuade and guide the congregation because they are responsible for the spiritual condition of the members.

Their appointment is not one of power, but one of responsibility. God will require them to give an account of every lost soul. As David pulled a lamb out of the mouth of a lion, so God will expect elders to rescue the wandering and weak members from the mouth of sin (1 Sam. 17:34-37). God expects elders to seek out and gather lost Christians. They are to be watched and protected, not ignored and neglected.

Awareness

Awareness is another part of oversight/attention. Paul charged the elders to give attention to and watch over the congregation as he had done (Acts 20:28,

31). Oversight meant being aware of the dangers that threaten a congregation. It also meant being aware of a member's temptation to stray. While Christians today are becoming more individualistic, there is a need for elders to recognize those who are drifting away in their church attendance, small group attendance, or attitudes. Seeking those who have drifted away and trying to bring them back involves awareness and attentiveness.

God is aware of the spiritual condition of people. While Israel lived in Egypt, God was aware of the children's suffering and struggles (Ex. 2:24; 3:8). God watched over and was concerned about the people during this slavery in Egypt (3:16; 4:31). God also protected Israel from the plagues (8:22-23) and from war so that they would not be discouraged (13:17). God knew the condition of Israel, saw their distress, and responded appropriately.

Visitation

Visitation is another way to manifest God's leadership. In the Hebrew and Greek Scriptures, God's visitation indicated that his people experienced or encountered the divine. The visitation of God was the presence of the creator to judge or redeem people. Elders who visit and meet with the members reflect an encounter with the divine through an encounter with God's anointed servant (Acts 20:28). Personal contact with Christians encourages them to experience the presence of God, as in the incarnation.

God visited his people so that he could validate their struggles and suffering. Israel was able to worship God because he had validated their condition by acknowledging their pain.

Empowerment

Finally, empowerment is also a part of care and concern for the congregation. While God appointed men to help Israel, he also sent men to accomplish his judgment. Delegation and punitive leadership were methods *Yahweh* used to attend to the flock. Elders have been gifted by Christ to enable/empower the congregation to mature and become involved in ministry, *diakonos* (Eph. 4:11-16).[70] While we many times have understood this work to mean service, the word also suggests administration, involvement, or acting as a go-between. Ministry involves members working together to build up the body of Christ and reach into the community with good works (Eph. 2:10; Titus 2:14). Those with different leadership gifts can work together to help the elders practice oversight in the church.[71] This delegation empowers or equips others in the congregation to use their gifts to grow and develop spiritually.

God's attention and concern reflects an involvement and awareness of the spiritual condition of Christians in the flock. The responsibility of elders to oversee the congregation involves being accountable to God, being aware of spiritual problems, visiting people to encourage them, and appointing others to continue to strengthen them in the faith.

GOOD SHEPHERDS MODEL GOD'S STYLE OF LEADERSHIP: RELATIONAL LEADERSHIP

The second part of incarnational leadership is shepherding. Shepherding is a relational method of leadership.[72] Elders have the responsibility to shepherd the flock by developing relationships among and with the congregation. While it is impossible for elders of large congregations to have intimate relationships with all members, they can see that members develop relationships among themselves. Elders can focus on areas that are highly relational and missing in many congregations. From my discussions with other ministers and elders, I find that elders can develop members and themselves through faith development and teaching (Eph. 4:11-16; 1 Tim. 3:2; Titus 1:9), practicing conflict resolution (Phil. 4:1-2), practicing hospitality (Rom. 12:13; 1 Tim. 3:2; Titus 1:8), and setting a spiritual example for the church (1 Peter 5:3; Heb. 13:7).

Faith Development and Teaching

Incarnational leadership leads to faith development and teaching. Elders can be attentive to the educational small group, and ministry programs that develop faith in the congregation. Taking responsibility for members' placement in some of these programs can ensure that many of them will develop their faith and relationships in the church. While personal faith development is strictly up to each individual Christian, guiding them to programs and ministries will provide them with opportunities to grow and mature in their faith. Elders should take initiative in encouraging ministers, teachers, deacons, or other members to create programs that develop these areas of the Christian life. Christians can develop stronger faith when they have leaders who guide them to spiritual growth.

> Pastoral care consists of all the ways a community of faith, under pastoral leadership, intentionally sponsors the awakening, shaping, rectifying, healing, and ongoing growth in vocation of Christian persons and community under the pressure and power of the in-breaking kingdom of God.[73]

Conflict resolution

Incarnational leadership leads elders to have strategies for conflict resolution. Congregations experience conflict because they consist of human beings. Fallenness is a part of our human conscience, and the devil encourages strife and controversy (1 Cor. 3:3; Gal. 5:20). Elders should shepherd by resolving conflict within the congregation. Paul encouraged the church to help Euodia and Syntyche agree in the Lord (Phil. 4:2).[74] Paul also challenged the church at Corinth to settle disputes within themselves rather than using the Roman legal system (1 Cor. 6:1-6).[75] The congregation was to practice harmony, reconciliation, and peace (Mt. 5:23; Eph. 4:1-6; Phil. 2:1-4).

Elders model God's leadership by guiding the congregation to resolve inner conflicts and to maintain peace and harmony within the covenant (Hosea 1-2; Rom. 5:6-8; 10:21). Elders imitate Christ, who brought peace and reconciliation (Eph. 2:14-15). God's willingness to forgive and re-establish covenants with people suggests that God is the master of conflict resolution and mediation (Hosea 2:20). The act of wooing the children in the wilderness and the humiliation of the cross are examples of God's willingness to be shamed in order to lead the people back (Hosea 2:14; Phil. 2:6-8; Col. 1:20).[76] God establishes rather than maintains peace. Reconciliation through mediation and conflict resolution are dimensions of relational leadership in the church.

Robert Sutton, a business professor at Stanford, has written extensively on the prevalence of bullies in corporations. According to Sutton these "jerks," a nicer term than he uses, cost companies thousands of dollars annually. They also affect employee morale, health and emotional welfare, and the reputation of the company. Whether these "jerks" are CEOs or regular employees, their difficult, abusive, and/or intimidating behavior has been ignored or tolerated by businesses for many years. Sutton's work challenges the mentality that seeks to keep these jerks on staff, because they may be productive or because it is hard to fire them. Keeping them around continues to promote an unhealthy environment for other employees.[77] Sutton calls for companies to take a stand and promote a "zero tolerance policy" for these bullies. It is the responsibility of business leaders to not allow this behavior in the company.

Sutton's work has tremendous implications for churches. Elders allow a staff member or another elder to continue to remain critical of other leaders. Elders are frustrated that other elders seem to resist the movement of the church, criticize (heavily) the preacher, or expect the minority to set the pace for the church. One or two elders dominate the ministry of the church. Younger elders are not empowered to lead.

Unfortunately, a common response to conflicts such as these has been to ignore the problem and wish it away. Sutton's research suggests action: elders and ministers have to work together to follow God's direction. Elders and ministers must not tolerate immature, controlling, or fear driven leaders. We need to cultivate a leadership that is open to being held accountable for God's vision. We need to cultivate a leadership that does not allow or expect the minority to rule. We need to cultivate a leadership that calls each other to act out of faith and love, not fear. We need leaders who have a zero tolerance for other controlling leaders.

Hospitality

Hospitality is a particular expectation of elders (1 Tim. 3:2). Hospitality is a mature Christian's duty and opportunity (Rom. 12:13).Hospitality in the Greco-Roman culture was practiced as a method of gaining favors in the patron/client system of the culture. Men would have clients as their servants or debtors who spent much of their time paying back favors by giving honor and praise to their "patrons." Hospitality was necessary in order for the head of the family (*patria familia*) to continue to be respected by the people. The Greek historian, Homer, suggested that the wealthy invite only their family, friends, and business associates to dinner. This way they could secure favors and receive a reciprocal invitation.

In early Christianity, hospitality was a way of accepting people who were not part of the "in group" and welcoming them into the spiritual family.[78] Elders were to lead in this method of evangelism and outreach to outsiders as well as to those in the household of God.

The Greek historian, Homer, suggested that the wealthy invite only their family, friends, and business associates to dinner. This way they could secure favors and receive a reciprocal invitation. Jesus, on the other hand, called the church to invite the outcasts, poor, oppressed, and sick to the table (Luke 14). Since they could not return the favor, God would repay them. At the heart of Christianity is a desire to reach out to others who need help, the love of a healthy family, and hospitality. Elders practice this hospitality by being open to strangers. This involves evangelism, being friendly to visitors at church, and opening their homes to members and others needing a place of protection.

For all this, the word "hospitality" has lost its moral punch over recent centuries. Reduced to connoting refreshments at meetings or magazine covers of gracious living, the moral landscape in which it resides has all but faded into the background. Yet it is this moral and spiritual landscape that early Christian voices can help us recover. Hospitality is characterized by a particular moral stance in the world that can best be described as readiness. Early Christian voices tell us again and again that whether we are guest or host we must be ready, ready to welcome, ready to enter another's world, ready to be vulnerable . . . for those who participate in hospitality, a de-centering of perspective occurs. In the experience of hospitality both the host and the guest encounter something new, approaching the edge of the unfamiliar and crossing it. Hospitality shifts the frame of reference from self to other to relationship.[79]

Hospitality involves a love of strangers and openness to the community, which suggests that the elder is both approachable and compassionate and initiates relationship with others.

Setting an Example

Finally, incarnational leadership sets an example of spirituality for the congregation. Peter told the elders to be "examples for the flock" (1 Peter 5:3). Elders strengthen their congregations by becoming models of God's justice and mercy. *Yahweh's* justice and righteousness were social issues. God was the protector of the poor and oppressed. God had a relationship with the afflicted and alien. The afflicted is also translated "humble" in the Greek Old and New Testaments. Jesus was humble (Mt. 11:28-30; Phil. 2:7-9), and he associated with the humble (Mt. 25; Luke 5:30; 7:34). To be humble, just, and righteous means that we become advocates for and associate with those who are oppressed by our society (Rom. 12:16).[80] Elders, who are examples of the Good Shepherd, are men who represent all people and show justice and mercy. All members of the congregation can come to them because they know that they are gentle and compassionate.

Elders imitate God relationally by developing the faith of other Christians, resolving conflict among members, visiting, and opening their homes and hearts to others. This transparency allows them to develop relationships with other Christians and helps them to become more effective as shepherds. An atmosphere of trust is developed in this type of congregation that allows Christians to grow spiritually and emotionally.

CONCLUSION

God's leadership is both organizational and relational. As a bishop, God is attentive and empowers people. God shepherds them in a compassionate relationship. Leaders follow God's example by leading with the same attention and passion. Ancient Israel failed in areas of leadership because they refused to imitate God (Jer. 23:1-4). The leaders in Ezek. 34:1-16 abused and neglected the sheep of Israel. God intervened and restored the lost sheep with oversight and compassion. Jesus imitated God's methods of leadership to a people who were sheep without a shepherd. Jesus commissioned his apostles to lead as he had. Peter and Paul trained men to imitate God's form of leadership by serving as shepherds and overseers.

Incarnational leadership has one main focus: to imitate God's method of leadership and reflect his concern and compassion to the people of God. This focus is empowered by the Holy Spirit through giftedness and divine appointment (Eph. 4:11; Acts 20:28).

QUESTIONS

1. What are the four components of Shawchuch and Heuser's model for transforming a church?

2. How can elders work with this model?

3. What are the two methods that God uses to lead people?

4. How do elders imitate God's model for the church and the world?

5. How can elders empower members to grow and develop spiritually?

Chapter 4

Baaaaaad Shepherds: Dysfunctional Leadership in the Kingdom

My wife, Lori, and I work with domestic violence victims and abusers in our ministry to Portland. This has had a tremendous effect on our marriage. We have learned that seeing dysfunction and learning how to address it can make a healthy relationship stronger. We believe this because we know what does and does not work in a marriage. We also observe what can destroy a covenant that was made in love but has become dysfunctional through violence, abuse, and other sin.

While some are uncomfortable with the term "dysfunctional" it is used by family counselors, therapists, and psychologists. This term exists because they acknowledge that certain behavior is unhealthy, morally wrong, and deeply destructive to "healthy" families and individuals. The faith community has been slow to take this type of stance. I conduct clergy trainings for sexual assault and abuse agencies locally as well as in other parts of the country. I also teach a seminary class designed to help clergy address these areas in the faith community and cities. The pattern has been consistent within all faith communities. We tend to turn our heads to abuse, dysfunction, and sin because we are not willing to take a stand for healthy relationships. It seems that we also rely on the crutch of "imperfection" as an excuse to avoid challenging others, as well as ourselves, to be what God has called us to be.

There are distinctions between dysfunctional and healthy families. Dysfunctional families do not address their destructive issues and patterns of behavior while healthy families are willing to correct the dysfunction and make a conscious effort to change. The assumption that this dysfunction exists because we live in a fallen world ignores the reality that we are part of a resurrected kingdom. The misquoting of Romans 3:23, "All have sinned" therefore we are all sinners, fails to acknowledge that the text (as well as the letter to the Romans) is calling the church to righteousness. Paul tells us that "all have sinned" (past tense) and later says that we "are justified/righteous" (present tense) in Jesus. Rather than enable dysfunction to continue to destroy a family, the faith community must intervene and call the family to health and wholeness.

DYSFUNCTIONAL LEADERSHIP

The same is true with leadership. When we see the dynamics of and damage caused by dysfunctional leadership, we know what destroys people and causes distrust among congregations and leaders. We can learn how to be healthier in our own relationships by observing unhealthy relationships.

Dysfunctional leadership exists when those with authority use their power to control others. Rather than empowering others to be what God calls them to be they manipulate and coerce people to do what the leaders wants. Dysfunctional leadership is dominated by fear—fear of outsiders, fear of "the world," fear of the future, fear of women, and fear of losing control. When 1 John 4:8 tells us that there is no fear in love, John suggests that God's love and leadership is healthy and empowering.

In this letter John is calling the church to remain in God. "Remain" (*meno*) occurs twenty four times. John compares this with the "world" which is temporary or passing away. Rather than allowing hatred for each other to become an issue in the church, John calls those who "hate their brother/sister" liars and outsiders. However, in 1 John 4 we are told that those who love (*agape*) live in God. There is no fear in those who live in God. Love empowers, love trusts, and love is not interested in controlling others. Love lets those who want to leave, go, and love causes them to encourage others to grow. Dysfunctional leaders, however, are dominated by fear rather than love. They resort to fear and control because they do not love and trust others to manifest the Spirit of God. They are anxious that others, who disagree with them, are not equally led by God's Spirit.

Dysfunctional leadership is similar to abuse in the family. Abuse is not about anger; it is about power and control.[81] Abusers control women because they do not respect them, and they feel that there is a competition for power. Shared power does not exist in an abusive marriage or family. Abusers are also highly narcissistic and have low self-esteem. This personal dysfunction causes them to be distant from others, especially those who threaten them—women. The relationship that they have with a woman fulfills a need for power and self love and causes the woman to empty herself so that the abuser can gain control of the relationship. He becomes an emotional vacuum. He is not one who operates out of love but fear.

Neglect is also a characteristic of an abuser. Whether together or separated, the abuser is not attentive to the needs of his family because he believes that they exist to serve and honor him. He also fails to validate his family's feelings through confession, repentance, and a change of behavior. In his mind it is their responsibility to "get over it." This neglect has been proven to cause trauma on developing the children's and partner's self-esteem. He neglects his family because he seeks to have his needs met rather than those of his family. Through neglect he holds power. His wife and children constantly wonder why he ignores them, and they, in turn, empty themselves to get his attention. Children are also more severely damaged by the tremendous power differential existing between themselves and significant adults.[82]

Dysfunctional leadership, as with abuse, involves using power and control to subordinate the flock. Dysfunctional leaders expect unquestioned obedience, submission, and respect. They neglect the flock by failing to confess, repent, or remove themselves from leadership when they fail. They will use whatever it takes to coerce members to follow them. They love the position more than the people. They also need the position and power because of their own selfishness and lack of self-esteem. They do not have a strong relationship with the members, but they expect them to submit without question. They also instill a sense of codependence in the members. Members believe that they have nowhere else to go and must stay in the church for their salvation and health. These leaders are dominated by fear, not a love that reflects God.

Again drawing a parallel between family and leadership—dysfunction is also reflected in the personality of victims. Victims of abuse are afraid, confused, and question their own insight and opinions. They struggle to think and to listen to themselves. Self blame and low self-esteem are the most common characteristics of victims. Abused wives suffer from post traumatic stress disorder (PTSD) and have a high rate of depression. Children of abusers also exhibit PTSD. The children model either the behavior of the abuser (aggression, manipulation, anger, control) or the victim (passivity, low self respect, fear, confusion). The fruits of the children are many times a reflection of the dysfunction in the home.

The emotional and spiritual health of a church is also reflected by its membership. Dysfunctional leaders may believe that control, coercion, fear, or manipulation is acceptable, but how the members feel about themselves is what we need to explore. Dysfunctional leaders do not listen nor do they worry about where the members need to be. They are focused on where they themselves want to be and where *they want/expect the members to be*. Dysfunctional leaders do not choose the ministry that best helps the members. They expect the members to become solely what they as the "authority" wants in ministry.

Dysfunctional leaders do not empower the church to be the best it can be. Dysfunctional leaders do not attend to the needs of people. Dysfunctional leaders neglect, control, and abuse their flock. Dysfunctional leaders are narcissistic and insecure. This type of leadership does not develop healthy relationships with the members. This type of leadership is clearly condemned in the prophets. The Jews were taken into captivity because their leaders were corrupt. In Jeremiah 23:1-4, God told the prophet to say:

"Woe to the shepherds who are destroying and scattering the sheep of my pasture!" declares *Yahweh*. Therefore this is what *Yahweh*, the God of Israel, says to the shepherds who shepherd my people: "Because you have scattered my flock and driven them away and have not cared for them, I will punish you for the evil you have done," declares *Yahweh*. I myself will gather the remnant of my flock out of all the countries where I have driven them and will bring them back to their pasture, where they will be fruitful and increase in number. I will place shepherds over them who will shepherd them, and they will no longer be afraid or terrified, nor will any be missing," declares *Yahweh*.

What were the shepherds doing wrong? First, they did not shepherd (*ra'h*) the sheep. Second, they did not care for or give attention to (*pqd*) the sheep. This word is used three times in the text. The shepherds do not *pqd*, but God will *pqd*, and therefore the sheep will be *pqd*. In this text the leaders failed to take care of the nation of Israel. In other prophets the shepherds deserted the flock or fell asleep on duty (Zech. 11:17; Is. 56:11). Because of this neglect, the people were driven into the wilderness (Jer. 10:21). There they wandered away from God. There they became easy prey for evil. There they fell into idolatry. God blamed the shepherds for the state of the nation because they had neglected the sheep.

What was God's solution—God would shepherd them (Jer. 23:3; Zech. 10:3). In Isaiah God promised to call them out and carry the sheep (40:11; 49:10). *Yahweh* displayed a sense of gentleness and concern for the lost sheep. God modeled healthy leadership. God gave them good shepherds (Jer. 23:4). When the sheep are shepherded, they are not afraid and they *grow and reproduce*!

If we want churches to grow, we must begin with leadership. When leadership wrongly uses power, they manipulate, intimidate, and control those who trust them. People living in a dysfunctional and abusive system cannot grow and develop in a healthy manner. They are afraid, confused, abused, and neglected. Healthy leadership, however, reflects God's oversight and care. Healthy leadership gives attention to the members. Healthy leadership empowers disciples to grow and reproduce because they are loved and live without fear. Leaders who reflect God's nature will bring healing to the flock.

Baaaaaaad Shepherds in Israel: Ezekiel 34

Dysfunctional Leadership and Israel

Defining attentive and relational leadership is an important step in the process of imaging God's leadership style. God's style of leadership involves both attention (oversight) and relationship (shepherding). The Scriptures reveal this style so that God's elders might imitate the divine nature by guiding the creation and the Kingdom. God is perfect, but man is not. God's leadership is a pattern that man could follow, but because of sin, Israel fell short of this pattern.

> The word of *Yahweh* came to me, "Son of man, prophesy against the shepherds of Israel; prophesy and say to them, 'This is what the sovereign Lord says: Woe to the shepherds of Israel who only take care of themselves. The shepherds should take care of the flock. You eat the curds, use the wool for clothes and slaughter the best animals, but you do not care for the flock. You have not strengthened the weak or healed the sick or bound up the injured. You have not brought back the strays or searched for the lost. You have ruled them harshly and brutally. So they were scattered because there was no shepherd, and when they were scattered they became food for all the wild animals. My sheep wandered over all the mountains and on every high hill. They were scattered over the whole earth, and no one searched or looked for them."

> "Hear the word of *Yahweh* you shepherds. As I live," declares sovereign *Yahweh*, "because my flock does not have a shepherd and so has been plundered and become food for all wild animals, because my shepherds did not search from my flock but cared for themselves rather than for my flock, therefore, shepherds, hear the word of *Yahweh*. This is what sovereign *Yahweh* says: I am against the shepherds and will hold them accountable for my flock. I will remove them

from shepherding the flock so that the shepherds can no longer feed themselves. I will rescue my flock from their mouths, and it will no longer be food for them."

This is what sovereign *Yahweh* says, "I will search for my sheep and care for them." (Ezek. 34:1-11)

This *fallenness* is illustrated by the critique of the shepherds/leaders in Ezekiel 34. The Israelite leaders were condemned for their failure to imitate God's leadership methods.[83] They have failed to practice oversight because they neglected the flock.[84] The leaders gave attention to themselves (34:2-3) and neglected the sheep (34:4).[85] The leaders also failed to practice relational leadership by neglecting the injured and stray sheep. The leaders did not strengthen the weak, heal the sick, bind up the injured, bring back the strays, and search for the lost. They were harsh in their treatment of God's people (34:4).[86] Because of their selfishness and neglect the sheep were scattered and open to predators (34:5-6).[87] God was angry because these leaders were given the responsibility to care for God's sheep. Since God guided, fed, nurtured, and protected the people, the leaders were expected to do the same. Israelite leadership failed to imitate God's care and concern for the people and as a result God's people strayed from the faith.[88]

God's Intervention and Healthy Model

God then intervened into this dysfunctional system through a *divine initiative*. First, God held the shepherds accountable for their actions, destroyed the strong, and judged the leaders (Ezek. 34:10, 16, 17-22). They were removed from leadership in order to rescue the sheep (34:10). God also sought out the stray sheep (34:11-14).[89] God was practicing oversight and a willingness to painstakingly search out the needs of the flock.

Second, God promised to bind the injured and strengthen the weak (Ezek. 34:15). *Yahweh's* oversight and care would strengthen the weak and judge the strong. God promised to restore the sheep by searching for the lost and shepherding them with justice (34:15-17). God would provide for their needs and care for them rather than oppress them. God showed how this style was to be done.

While this may have referred to the Babylonian captivity and restoration, God did promise to place a new shepherd over them. This *salvation* would be displayed by the Davidic shepherd who was to establish a covenant of peace, safety, and knowledge of *Yahweh* (Ezek. 34:23, 25, 28, 30).[90] While this Davidic shepherd led them as Judah returned from captivity, the hope for another Davidic shepherd was present in the first century AD. Jesus claimed to be this type of shepherd. He called himself the "good shepherd" who overthrew the hirelings and thieves (John 10:11, 18). The good shepherd, Jesus, laid his life down for the sheep and was concerned about their needs. God again saved the flock through the incarnation of Christ. Salvation in Jesus is also God's intervention and provision of a healthy leader to shepherd the members.

Sanctification occurred as God empowered leaders to imitate this style of leadership. Jesus called Peter to imitate God's style when He challenged Him to "shepherd" or "feed my sheep" (John 21:15, 16, 17).[91] Peter also challenged elders to shepherd God's flock willingly and as examples (1 Peter 5:2-3). The verbs in this text suggest a pattern of behavior that the apostle wants the church to model.[92] J. Ramsey Michaels points out that Peter contrasts the styles of Christian leadership with the current cultural styles. The elder is to shepherd intentionally rather than out of compulsion or force.[93] Elders are to shepherd eagerly rather than out of greed.[94] Elders are to set an example instead of ruling with force.[95] Peter reminded the elders that they were accountable to the chief shepherd (5:4) and that the flock was an inheritance given to them (5:2). The responsibility to shepherd with God's method was placed by God upon the leaders. They were to lead by example and persuasion, not by coercion and force.

Paul reminded the elders that the Holy Spirit had made them leaders (Acts 20:28).[96] Paul equally challenged elders to lead as God did. He also wrote that shepherds were gifts given to the church by Christ (Eph. 4:7-11). God empowered elders to lead by placing them in authority through the Holy Spirit and their giftedness. Through this, the flock is cared for, nurtured, and restored.

This theological framework indicates the failures of leadership in a fallen world. Neglect and abuse were consistent with Israel's sinfulness in their leaders. Peter warned the elders about abuse (1 Peter 5:3), and Paul warned them about neglecting the flock (Acts 20:28). The early church did not want their leaders to imitate the sinfulness of the leaders in Israel (Ezek. 34). God intervenes by modeling healthy shepherding. This style is seen in Jesus, who was the chief shepherd. Jesus, like *Yahweh*, also intervened calling leaders to accountability and empowering them to imitate God's care and concern for the flock. Incarnational leadership brings sanctification to a nation suffering from *baaaaaaad* shepherds!

GOOD SHEPHERDS

From the texts of the prophets, one understands that dysfunctional or abusive leadership involves neglect, control, and coercion of people. God intervened and confronted these leaders through the prophets. God intervened and confronted these leaders through the prophets. God continued to intervene by modeling leadership in the ministry of Jesus. The Spirit intervenes through the word, call to repentance, and by empowering leaders to shepherd like God. God expected these leaders to uphold a standard of care, compassion, and respect for the nation of Israel. Leaders were to love the flock as God loved them and were to empower them to grow and be at peace. The same is true today. Too often I hear that we are to accept that leaders are human and flawed or that we need to be patient with them. This "sense of fallenness" may be true. God, however, has set a standard for leaders, and we are to hold them to that standard. Leaders are to uphold God's standards and show the congregation what it means to live like Jesus. Dysfunctional leadership is unacceptable to God, and the prophets were called to confront these leaders.

Does God's grace cover dysfunctional leadership? Those who sin can be forgiven, but there must be repentance. Those who sin also can affect others. Leaders who sin can be forgiven, but there must be repentance. That repentance may involve validating those people who have been hurt by the leaders' sins.

The issue is repentance. How do leaders repent? Actually the question that should be asked is, "How much damage has been done when leadership is dysfunctional or abusive?" Just as an abuser needs to spend months/years committing to change, participating in intervention groups, and validating his victims so leaders may need to spend months/years "bearing fruits of repentance" (Matt. 3:8). Just as the Jews had to spend seventy years in Babylonian captivity, leaders may have to step down permanently. Many church leaders have caused damage to members, their community, and the reputation of Jesus in that community.

As a result some leadership issues may take one or two generations before the community heals (although people are never completely healed). Sometimes it takes other leaders, such as righteous Daniel, to acknowledge the sins of the fathers and publicly repent before God. Whether we like it or not, the sins of leadership run deep and repentance of those sins is a complex process. This is why healthy leadership is so needed in our congregations. Grace is possible, but repentance is necessary. This is why God sends prophets to leaders of the community.

"*Yahweh* sent Nathan to David . . ." (2 Sam. 12:1). Just as Nathan confronted King David, God confronts dysfunctional leaders today. David was not the best model for leadership. David's family was a family in turmoil, sin, and injustice. While David was a man after God's heart, it was Josiah who was the greatest king and the one who followed God's law (2 Kings 23:25). David not only murdered his best warrior (Uriah) he sexually harassed and coerced Bathsheba (Uriah's wife). He abused his power as a leader on many levels. In the end his violence kept him from building a temple to God and he experienced these same sins in his own family.

God confronted David so that we would know that God does not turn a deaf ear to those oppressed by sinful leaders. While we must understand that leaders are human, they are *expected* to bear fruits of the Spirit. Leaders are *expected* to model and reflect God. When they fail they may damage many others. Leadership is not a place for immature people. Leadership is not a place for selfish people. Leadership is not a place for those led by fear. Leaders will be held accountable for their actions and the damage that they cause.

"No one is perfect!" True, but one issue that we need to address in healthy leadership is maturity. The word translated *perfect* or *complete* in many of our texts (Matt. 5:48; 1 Cor. 13:10), *telos*, is actually translated mature in other biblical texts (Eph. 4:11-16; Phil. 3:15). I think that our language needs to be consistent in these texts:

> Matt. 5:48 = God is *mature* because God loves enemies. I need to be mature like God. Luke 6:36 tells us to be merciful like God is merciful.

> Eph. 4:13 = Leaders help the church to become *mature* and not stay as infants. Immature people do not help others mature.

> 1 Cor. 13 = Love is *mature* because it seeks the benefit of others. Paul grew up and became a man (mature) and put away childish things. When love comes, the church will not need to focus on immature gifts (tongues/languages) but it can give and encourage others through prophesy.

> Col. 3:14 = Above all of these put on love, which binds everything together in *mature/perfect* harmony.

> Col. 4:12 = Epaphras, who is one of you, a servant of Christ Jesus, greets you, always struggling on your behalf in his prayers, that you may stand *mature* and fully assured in all the will of God.

Perfection is unattainable, but maturity is both *attainable* and *expected*. Leadership is expected to be mature, by both God and the people. While maturity is not perfection, mature Christians do not use sin, fear, and weakness as an excuse. Mature people try to put away sin (Eph. 4:25-5:2; Col. 3:5-16), reflect the fruit of the Spirit (Gal. 5: 16-26), are led by the Spirit (Rom. 8:5), and aim to grow close to God (Phil. 3:12-15). Mature Christians practice sacrificial love (1 Cor. 13-14) with those inside the faith and those outside who are lost (Phil. 2:1-8). Jesus was the friend of sinners and tax collectors—He is the model of our maturity (Luke 7:34). Mature Christians do not make excuses for sin, but they prove by their life and longevity that repentance does produce change and transformation.

Good shepherds are to be mature Christians, not flawless. They must be mature so that they can lead the congregation to maturity. Leaders cannot be narcissistic, abusive, or neglectful of the church. They practice *agape* love. They have relationship and practice oversight because they are concerned about the needs of the congregation and deeply love people.

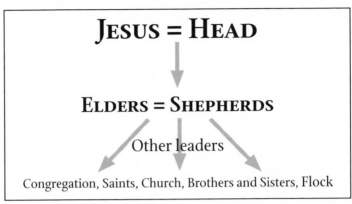

Figure 3—Traditional Diagram for Elders

Good shepherds are also team players. While we acknowledge Jesus as head, leaders may still adopt a hierarchy over the rest of the congregation. Hierarchies may not necessarily be bad but Jesus tells us that leadership is about service, not a place of order or a scale that ranks where people should be in a structure. While I understand that Figure 3 tended to be an action model for elders to work with the church, it still suggests a hierarchy, or top down, method of leadership. Post modern culture; whether we like it or not, will strongly react to any picture that suggests people being "over others." Hierarchies can cultivate an abuse of power or something that threatens free will, especially in our culture. Even though most first-century people lived under a hierarchy, Jesus chose a different method of ministry. Since ministry is about reaching people, a different picture must be sought out to empower leaders and members to do ministry.

I have also seen the model in Figure 3 inverted to suggest that the elders are at the bottom and serve/support the congregation, but the power of the leadership still resides in the elders (Figure 4). The elders are also expected to be the "greatest servants" of the church and many times become slaves of the congregation. At times this prevents elders and their wives from setting healthy personal boundaries and knowing "when to say no."

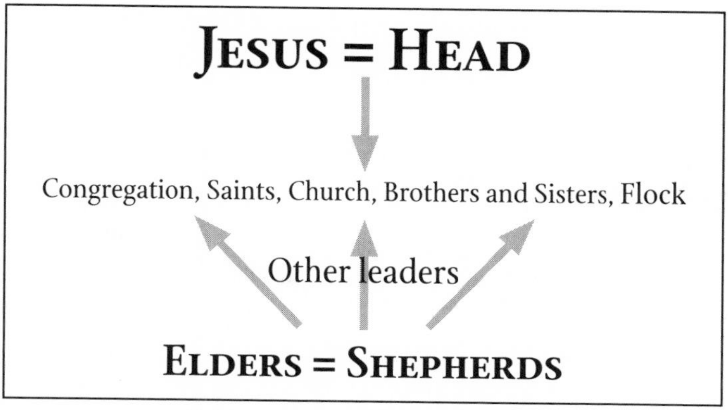

JESUS = HEAD

Congregation, Saints, Church, Brothers and Sisters, Flock

Other leaders

ELDERS = SHEPHERDS

Figure 4—Inverted Diagram for Elders

Incarnational leadership (Figure 5), however, reflects the Word/God becoming flesh and living among us. As God dwelt in the temple (tent and building), the congregation surrounded the holy place. As God dwelt in human form (John 1:1, 18), people encamped around the holy one and touched him (1 John 1:1-5). Incarnational leaders live and minister among the people. They emerge from the community to empower others to follow Jesus. Incarnational leadership exists among the people to empower them.

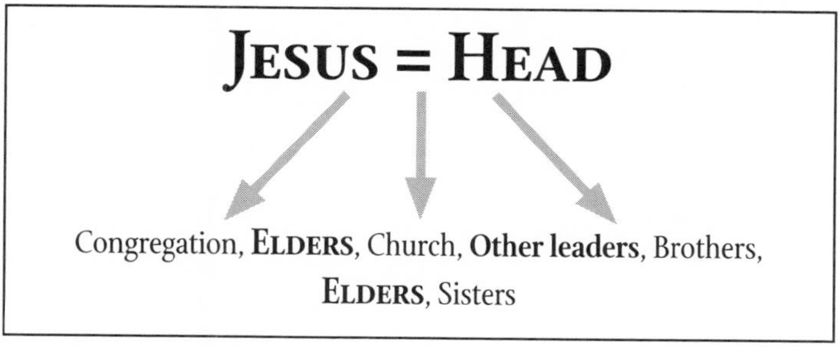

JESUS = HEAD

Congregation, **ELDERS**, Church, **Other leaders**, Brothers, **ELDERS**, Sisters

Figure 5—Incarnational Diagram for Elders

Elders who lead incarnationally work with God, the church, and other leaders to guide and develop members for growth and maturity. They use their giftedness and the giftedness of other leaders and members to reach their communities for Christ. They walk among the people, not above them, to lead them closer to God.

LEADERSHIP IN THE GRECO-ROMAN EMPIRE

Incarnational leadership is similar to the ancient Greek forms of democracy, leadership, and government. Greek city states were very democratic in their politics. Elected leaders of the city would "call the community out," forming an *ekklesia* (the Greek word for church). The leaders' responsibility was to inform the people and persuade them to vote on an issue.[97] The power of the leaders existed in their ability to use logic, passion, and character to persuade people to make right choices. The relationship that they had with their people was very influential and affected how their community worked to elect leaders and vote on issues.

The Romans, on the other hand, did not work democratically (except within the Senate). When the Greek city states were conquered by the Romans, the *ekklesia* no longer had the power once it had under the Greek government. Roman leaders were placed in the city to make decisions for the people, call them out, and inform them what Rome had decided. Archaeologists at Corinth have found the "Bema" place where the Roman proconsul sat and delivered judgments for the city. Paul refers to the Bema in 2 Corinthians 5:9 as God's throne and place of judgment. Paul, who had appeared before Gallio's Bema (Acts 18), is making an allusion to a location of which the Corinthians were familiar. Rome used the Bema to hand down decrees and inform the populace what was already decided. These cities did not have a democratic government, and the Roman leaders only needed approval from Caesar to convince the *ekklesia* to accept the Senate's decrees.

The church, at least for the first two centuries, did not use the Roman hierarchical style of leadership. Jesus refers to this when he says, "The kings (emperors) of the Gentiles lord it over them . . . but you are not to be like that . . . " (Luke 22:25-26). Christian leadership was to be counter-cultural to Roman leadership; however, the leadership of the early church was similar to that of the Greek democratic style. First, the *ekklesia* was asked to *select leaders* (Acts. 6:1-7). Second, *persuasion* (not submission) was the key ingredient for an effective leader in the church. "Remember your leaders, who spoke the word of God to you. Observe the outcome of their way of life [conduct] and *imitate their faith*" (Heb. 13:7; see also v. 17). Hebrews 13:7, 17 has typically been translated and used to enforce obedience and submission, yet it actually suggests listening, persuading, and supporting leaders. The emphasis is on the leader's character. The leader's character has a large affect on those who follow. Third, leaders were *not to lord it over the church*. They could not use power over others. Finally, leaders gathered churches to *inform them* and *ask them for feedback* (Acts 6: 1-6; 15; 20:7-12).

Leaders often say the kingdom of God is not a democracy. My response is no and yes. First, *God is in charge*—Jesus is the head. It is a kingdom. It is an Empire. Greek democracy was itself under the rule of Zeus and his pantheon. The gods were in charge, but the people elected religious leaders who empowered them (this was considered divine) to make right choices. Democracy existed under the council of the gods (who also discussed decisions). Leaders stilled feared the gods, if they believed in them, and operated under divine authority. Yet, the people worked with leaders to fulfill the will of the gods. While the church is the body of Christ and under his authority, this does not deny that democratic principles still exist.

Second, *the members and leaders exist as a democracy in which an effective leader uses their gifts of persuasion, rather than coercion*. While the church is part of the kingdom, the members work with leaders to grow and accomplish God's mission. Yet the most influential leaders are those who set a moral example and effectively persuade the church to make right choices. Respect is given to those with character, passion, and wisdom. While God has the right and authority to command respect as the creator, human leaders earn and develop respect by their character.

Third, *leaders do have authority from God*. They, at times, will have to confront those who threaten the flock. They will have to ask heretics or troublemakers to leave. They will have to take a stand on biblical and doctrinal issues. But they must do it in an atmosphere of trust and respect, not fear and control.

Conclusion

Elders are called by Jesus to lead incarnationally. Elders and their wives lead by example. Their moral character is such that people are not hesitant to trust them and follow their lead. They also empower the church to make right choices for God. They do this through persuasion rather than with a heavy hand. We must never forget that members can "vote with their feet." Dysfunctional leadership forces them to stay by creating fear, confusion, and doubt. Healthy leadership empowers members to make right choices and loves them as God loves all people. A congregation led by good shepherds will grow and develop in its community. Incarnational leadership is not about controlling others but about empowering them. Incarnational leadership persuades, guides, and develops members through trust, love, character, and a passion for Jesus.

QUESTIONS

1. How is dysfunctional leadership abusive?

2. How were the elders/shepherds in the Old Testament abusive?

3. What is healthy shepherding?

4. How do elders lead incarnationally?

5. What is your opinion of the proposed model of leadership, Figure 4? Explain why you agree or disagree.

6. Why is it important to understand *telos* as maturity rather than perfection?

Chapter 5

ELDERS AND THE SPIRIT

Healthy leadership involves empowering members to develop emotionally and spiritually. Healthy leadership depends on the character of the leaders. This character was necessary so that the early church could also reflect a holy lifestyle in the Roman culture. The early Christian movement needed to have a good reputation in the community. Roman authorities had the power to determine the legality of meetings, associations, or religious communities. To be branded *religio illicita* (illegal religion) would have been a bad mark on the Christian community. Therefore, the reputation and survival of the church was a key factor in the writings of the early church leaders.

This reputation came through the power of the Holy Spirit and was manifested by elders and other leaders. Elders had to be men who were led by the Spirit. They needed to reflect the power and fruits of the Spirit. The biblical text, unlike many ancient Near-eastern texts, gives us these spiritual qualities/qualifications for those who serve as elders.

1 Timothy and Elders

One of the most common texts used in elder development is 1 Tim. 3:1-7. In my experience, the text has been placed beside Titus 1:5-12 and the two merged to produce a checklist for the characteristics of elders. While this may develop a strong set of qualifications for elders, I think that it causes many to lose focus on the most important qualities, such as family and the personality of an elder. I think the differences between the two texts should instead highlight the specific situations at Crete and Ephesus.[98]

The Context of Ministry in the Pastorals

The major differences between the two texts can give us insight into issues that the churches faced. One major difference between the texts is that Titus was to find men whose children were believers, but Timothy did not have this instruction. The other difference was that Timothy was instructed not to appoint a new convert yet, Titus was not given this exclusion. Why are there these differences? I believe that we can examine the contexts of the letters and cultures answer this question.

Timothy was working with the church in Ephesus, which was an established church that had elders and had been around for a few years.[99] Timothy's main function seems to be to prepare the elders to meet Paul (Acts 20:17), who sent him to Ephesus (Acts 20:1-6) in order to appoint more elders and strengthen the established church. It is also likely that Paul was using the letter to Timothy to communicate to the Ephesian church that Timothy was his successor while he was absent.[100]

The letter to Titus, on the other hand, gives us an indication that the church was fairly new.[101] In Titus 1:5, Paul left Titus on Crete to appoint elders, a task he had obviously been neglecting. From passages in the text (1:12-16; 3:9-10), it seems that Titus was getting caught in arguments about the law. Zenas, the lawyer, and Apollos were to be sent to Paul (3:13) and it is most likely that Titus felt he had to carry on their ministry and debate with those discussing the Jewish law (3:9). Paul encouraged him to appoint elders (that was why he was sent), call the people to morality, and prepare to leave. Titus was to be replaced by Artemas and Tychicus (3:12). Titus had a purpose, which was to quickly appoint elders.

It also seems that the church on Crete was new because the elders were struggling with sin. The immorality on Crete was bad, and the elders needed to be challenged (1:13). Both Timothy and Titus were addressing similar issues within the church and culture but they were specific to each church. Paul was also communicating to the Cretan and Ephesian communities that Timothy and Titus were both his successors, and that they carried his authority in their ministry for Christ.[102]

Since the Cretan church was relatively new, any appointed elder would have been new. Titus, Artemas, and Tychicus would have provided a consistent training program for the elders to help them grow. The church at Ephesus, however, already had elders as well as converted Jews who could minister (Acts 18:26) and carry on the teachings of Jesus.

Another difference between the two letters was the requirement for children. Titus was told to find men whose children believe (Titus 1:6). This would be necessary in a culture steeped in idolatry and paganism, especially one where fathers molested their own boys (such as in Crete). Yet Timothy was only told to appoint men whose children respected and obeyed him (1 Tim. 3:4).

Ephesus was an established church with a strong Jewish community. It seems that elders who had children who respected them and were obedient could serve well in this area.[103] Family conversions in Acts suggest to us that the future leaders of the church first led their families to the Lord. For Titus, an elder needed believing children. For Timothy, the Ephesian elders could serve as long as their children were respectful and obedient to their father. It seems that a man in Ephesus with respectful children could serve, but at Crete a man needed his whole household converted to the faith for him to serve. This would have set a good family example to the Cretan community and prevented the harsh divisions that would have occurred in a divided home.

Traditionally, we have merged the qualifications of Titus and 1 Timothy and suggested, to be safe, that elders not be new converts and that their children must be believers in the faith. We have little authority to do this. The problem with this interpretation is that it excludes some men from shepherding where Paul and Jesus would expect them to serve in this position. An elder at Crete might not be able to be an elder in Ephesus or our churches, and vice versa. An elder in first century Ephesus might not be able to be an elder in one of our churches. The texts indicate that in "some contexts" a man can be an elder even if his children do not all believe in Jesus. In "some contexts" a man who is a fairly recent convert can be an elder of a church.

A Note About Believing Children and Parents

Over the years I have worked in youth ministry and ministry in small churches. One issue that continues to permeate our thinking concerns children of believers leaving the church. If a child grows up in the church and later chooses to leave the church (falls away) instead of working to restore the child or find out what is wrong, we blame the parents. Somehow we suggest that the parents failed to raise the child properly. We are similar to Eliphaz who suggests that Job's children died because Job must have sinned (Job. 5:3-4). Yet we fail to see the pain that we further inflict on those already grieving and searching for answers.

The same is true concerning elders. A man cannot become an elder, in some churches, if any of his children are not active in the church (which many would suggest can only be an Restoration Movement church). However, is this actually biblical or even a logical application? Is it possible that a couple can raise their children in a Christian home only to find that a child or children can grow to choose to leave the faith? Is God to blame when people walk away and violate the covenant? Are elders to blame for those in the church who one day chooses to leave the community? Is a spouse to blame when the other chooses to become unfaithful or dysfunctional and violate the marriage covenant? Does free will play a part in anyone's decision?

First, I remember suggesting to some evangelists, in Mexico, that the unbelieving children be interviewed (as well as any other children) before a man is chosen to be an elder. Why did they leave? Did they choose of their own free will or did their parent's behavior influence this choice? Should their father be an elder? Is it possible that other Christian's immoral behavior influenced the children to leave? The response of the children would indicate what type of parent the church was working with. *It is possible that children of Christian parents make their own choice to leave a church.* The evangelist's response was, "We do not care what the ungodly have to say about spiritual matters."

Second, Proverbs 22:6 "Train up a children in the way they should go and when they are old they will not depart from it . . . " suggests to some that this applies to parenting. However, this is a poor application of the verse. I hold to the view that the Proverbs were similar to other forms of ancient Near Eastern Wisdom texts that were designed to be used in scribal schools to train young men for service in the court and community. They abound with justice, righteousness, and fairness words.[104] The word for youth (*naar*) is a word that suggests an apprentice, young man, or noble person. This would apply to a student, not a child. The text simply says that if a young person is introduced to a task or work (that fits them) they will not depart from that task. This is a text that suggests we apprentice young people by introducing them to something that they are skilled at doing—which provides them with a life occupation. *The text does not apply to raising children but to mentoring young men and women.*

Finally, *people make their own choices.* There are many elders' children who are apathetic and take up space in the church. Their presence in the faith community may say nothing about their faithfulness. This does not suggest that the parents were any better because their children go to a church. Parents are to train their children to make choices and part of that involves, sometimes allowing them permission to choose against their wishes. Just as we do not condemn God for allowing people to have free will, so we should not judge parents as able to lead due to the actions of their children. Any time a couple is considered to be leaders we should meet with the children and talk with them about their perspectives on parents. I have had unbelieving children support their parents as godly leaders and believing children suggest we do not put their parents in leadership. Their perspectives many times give us a good indication of what it means to manage and lead a family.

I believe we are extremely slow in appointing elders in mission churches and church plants. According to Titus (and some of the Syrian churches), it is possible to have elders appointed in a church plant by the second year of the church. It is also possible in a mission church to appoint men as elders in the second year of the church. The differences between Timothy and Titus give us examples where men can serve as elders, specific to their contexts. The differences also challenge us to view the importance of having elders as more important than the need for a man to fulfill every single qualification mentioned in both 1 Timothy and Titus. Furthermore, these are minor qualifications in my opinion.

While I do believe that all of God's word is important, I think that Jesus' point with the Pharisees is well taken. He accuses them of neglecting the "heavy" (important) matters (Matt. 23:23) of the law—justice, mercy, and faithfulness. Paul tells us that faith, hope, and love abide and that the greatest is love (1 Cor. 13:13). There are qualities and teachings that carry weight in our faith. Too often we neglect these issues and focus on those that are less important. My suggestion is that we have focused on the wife and children qualifications of elders to the neglect of the more important characteristics such as gentleness, peacemakers, etc. We have heavily focused on these qualifications to the neglect of the more important issues which will be discussed below.

Ephesus, Spirituality, and the Church

Historians consider Ephesus to be one of the most important cities in the Roman Empire. While the Christian churches met in homes, they dwelt under the Roman protective umbrella of "club" or "association."[105] Sometimes life under this umbrella was not supportive. The economic pressures were heavy in times of famine, sickness, or war. While Ephesus had a strong mix of Syrian and Roman cultures, their values and ethics were religiously oriented. Leaving a family religion for Jesus the Christ meant pressure from the family, employers, and trade unions with which one was associated (Acts 19:23-41). While the Jews had won their right to be monotheistic, Christianity was only safe while it was considered a branch of Judaism. When the Jews turned on the Christians, the church was persecuted. Christianity later became *religio illicita*. Christians had freedom to assemble until their community turned against them. They then became suspect.

Paul was concerned that the churches carry a good reputation in their Roman culture. Notice in letters to Timothy and Titus Paul's emphasis on having a good conscience, healthy teaching, being an example, and doing good deeds.

Paul wanted the Christians to live peaceful lives, which entailed men leading and women being submissive. The church needed to set an example in the world. "The goal of our instruction is love from a pure heart and a good conscience and sincere faith." The early Christians were going to change the world by being examples to the world, showing the morality of Christ, and being loyal citizens. In the midst of pressure and persecution, they would overcome through submission and faithfulness to God and man (Titus 2:11-14; Luke 2:52; Acts 2:47).

Paul's desire for the church was that they set a moral and respectful example for their neighbors and family. While the cost of following Jesus seemed to be an abandonment of one's social ties, Paul called the church to live in harmony with each other and their environment. While Cretan women were expected to manage their husband's home; therefore, Paul encouraged the women to continue to be examples in their community as caretakers in the home (Titus 2:5). He also encouraged women to support the cultural norms of being silent in the presence of men at the dinner table (1 Cor. 14:34). Paul believed that there was no law against those who practiced the fruits of the Spirit (Gal. 5:22-26). These fruits, however, must be present in the leaders of the church.

Elders Reflect Christ's Moral Nature

Timothy and Titus were called to appoint elders and call them to righteousness in order to help the church live a moral life in the Roman world.[106] If anyone wanted to be an elder and lead the church, he desired a good work. While desire is considered a requirement for an elder, the point of the text is that this is a good work (1 Tim. 3:1). This is a position that requires moral integrity (Titus 1:9). The elder is to be blameless or above reproach.[107] This is also a requirement for people in the church (1 Tim. 5:7; 6:14). All Christians are to try to be blameless. This is behavior that people can attain. I think that we enable immaturity in our leaders when we suggest that this word is unattainable. I believe that God does not call people to an impossible standard. If an elder is to be blameless, it is not an unattainable state. The elder is to live a life that does not bring shame on Christ, the church, and the gospel. In a world seeking to find fault with Christianity, the elder needed to live and reflect the faith and character of the Christian community.

Paul then lists characteristics in these Pastorals that define blameless-ness. He discussed personal characteristics such as being sober, self-controlled, modest, hospitable, and able to teach. The elder is neither a drunk nor violent or abusive, literally "not a bully," which means that he does not intimidate or misuse power), but he is gentle and peaceful and not greedy. The elder is also to love what is good and be disciplined (Titus 1:8).

Rarely have I heard of a man being removed from leadership for failures in these areas. Other than drunkenness, I have yet to see an elder disciplined for abusing these characteristics. Conversely, I rarely see praise for elders who dis-play these characteristics. These are behaviors that are difficult to teach. Men and their wives who display these qualities should be encouraged to train as shepherds. Morality, empathy, and compassion are difficult to teach adults. Therefore, leadership development programs should first seek out couples with these qualities as potential elder candidates. Men who struggle in these areas should be encouraged to focus on blamelessness, compassion, and empathy.

I have heard the term "personality issues" used when referring to these characteristics. When we work with abusive men we find out that these men struggle to express two qualities: empathy and compassion. As men we are not usually taught to freely express these qualities, especially by our fathers. Those who display compassion, gentleness, empathy, and peacefulness are sometimes viewed as female or homosexual, or emo (a term used by young people today for emotional people and effeminate males). The men who freely express these qualities have mainly been taught by women, feminists, or by their own mis-takes with anger, control, and rage. Ethicists suggest that what is lacking in our society is not only compassion and empathy, but the consideration that these are moral issues, rather than personality issues.

One interesting characteristic of the Proverbs is the emphasis on hear-ing the voice of females. While Proverbs 1-9 suggest a father (or school father/teacher) speaking to his son/students, overwhelmingly the female voice is prev-alent in the book. Wisdom is feminine. When compared to the foolish woman, prostitute, and adulteress she is worth more than money and everything that the youth can possess. The foolish woman, however, hollers and yells in the streets, lady Wisdom is quiet and calls to the young men because she "'aint no hollaback girl." The noble woman is not only Wisdom, but the woman worth marrying. At the end of the book, in chapter 31, King Lemuel's mother (momma Lemuel) gives two bits of advice to her son. First, defend the oppressed and afflicted (Prov. 31:8-9). Second, marry the noble woman because she cares for her family, the poor, and the oppressed (31:10ff). In this book compassion, justice, empathy, and mercy are ethics that the young man needs to succeed. They are the beginning of wisdom and represent the fear of *Yahweh* (1:7). Even more than this, he learns these moral qualities from a woman. Empathy and compassion, in the Proverbs, become the desire of the young apprentice. However, empathy and compassion were typically viewed as feminine in the ancient East.

Empathy and compassion are not personality characteristics. They are moral issues. Men must learn these when they are young. Why? In our work with abusers and sexual offenders we find that empathy and compassion are extremely difficult, if not impossible, to teach middle aged or older men. Statistically if men do not learn this as young boys they are unlikely to change, on their own, when they are older. The same is true of men in the church. Older men who do not practice the moral characteristics of empathy and compassion will have a difficult time changing. Our elderships cannot afford to have men who do not see these qualities as moral issue also must cultivate a congregation that expects this from men, especially male leaders.

Traditionally, I have noticed that when seeking elders we look for men who can teach, attend church regularly, and have a good working knowledge of the Bible. While these characteristics are important, they can be taught and learned relatively quickly. A person with an open heart can learn the Bible in a year with a good teacher. But a Bible scholar who does not open his home or who is not gentle will struggle for years to develop these qualities. Gentleness and peacefulness are fruits of the Spirit, and a man *must have* these and practice these in order to be considered for the position of elder.

Another important point concerns teaching. The elder is to be an apt teacher. In the ancient world teachers were not always "lecturers." Teaching involved persuasion. Aristotle suggested that effective speakers needed character (*ethos*), passion (*pathos*), and a logical argument (*logos*). These qualities worked together to persuade" the hearer to make a good choice. Persuasion involves character, relationship, passion, and a good argument. Apt teachers (*kalos didaskalia*, 1 Tim. 3:2) are not men who deliver a good speech; they are men whose words, lives, and passion can persuade people to make wise choices. In Titus, the elder must hold to the teaching of the word and be able to encourage others, by healthy teaching and living, and confront the immoral (Titus 1:9). Elders do not only lecture; they persuade others, by their lives, to grow in a relationship with Jesus.

Paul sought elders who let the Spirit of Christ control their lives. An elder who is harsh, rude, uncontrolled, bitter, and greedy will only destroy the church's reputation in the world. They will destroy people as they have destroyed themselves. Leaders who misuse power and resort to intimidation are not reflecting the fruits of the Spirit or the nature of God (Gal. 5:22-26; Exod. 34:6-7). Elders cannot be men who fail to practice meekness, compassion, gentleness, and peacefulness. These are the major issues of our faith and should be expected from all of our elders. If an elder is confronted for harshness, rudeness, arrogance, losing control, or intimidation, that person should discern whether this is true, and if so take sabbatical or resign and begin the process of repentance and redevelop his character to be like Jesus. These behaviors are not personality "glitches," they are spiritual issues. Words such as "good," "loving" "gentle," "compassionate," and "merciful," are most commonly used to describe Jesus and used by Paul to the church to indicate spiritual maturity. The moral characteristics that Paul suggests for an elder involve personality, integrity, compassion, and empathy. The actions of our elders and leaders will either honor or humiliate the church. Who we appoint will either help us continue in God's vision or will block it from our community.

Conclusion

Elders and their families reflect love, compassion, and courage to the church and community. Elders are seen as "good men" in their community. Their family loves them and is empowered by them to grow and develop. They model a life in and of the Spirit. They display compassion and empathy. They model this lifestyle so that the church can also become a light to a world struggling to find hope in darkness. The church will grow and mature with elders who model these character ethics. The church will also manifest the same nature to their communities. Empathy, compassion, love, gentleness, peacefulness are both needed and missing in our world today. They are the major issues that we must emphasize in leadership development.

QUESTIONS

1. What are the differences in 1 Tim. 3:1-8 and Titus 1:5-9?

2. Why do you think that these differences exist?

3. How does this affect elder development?

4. In your experience, have we neglected the "major issues" in elder development? Why or why not?

5. What does Jesus tell us that the major/weightier issues are (Matt. 23:23)?

6. What are spiritual areas that you need to strengthen in your life?

7. How will you strengthen them?

Chapter 6

ELDERS AND THEIR FAMILIES

I n the ancient world, family was an important vehicle for personal development. How a father guided his family was a reflection of his effectiveness as
a leader. Caesar Augustus called himself the "father of the state." He was seen as
the householder of Rome. The family and home were places of leadership, community, and acceptance. Leaders proved their character and leadership skills by
how they "managed" their homes and families.

> *Manage* the city as you would your ancestral estate: in the matter of
> its appointments, splendidly and royally, in the matter of its reve-
> nues, strictly, in order that you may possess the good opinion of your
> people. (Isocrates, *Ad Nicoclem* 19)

> Whenever you purpose to consult with any one about your affairs,
> first observe how he has *managed* his own; for he who has shown poor
> judgment in conducting his own business will never give wise counsel
> about the business of others. (Pseudo-Isocrates, *Ad Demonicum* 35)

> Yet they really desire any and every thing in preference to becoming
> good, and they busy themselves with everything in preference to the
> problem of becoming self-controlled and wise and righteous and men

of merit, competent to lead themselves well, to *manage* a household [family] well, to rule a city well, to endure well either wealth or poverty, to behave well toward friends and kinsmen, to care for parents with equity, and to serve gods with piety. (Dio Chrysostom, *On Virtue* 69:2)

Organized communities are of two sorts, the greater which we call cities and the smaller which we call households. Both of these have their governors; the government of the greater is assigned to men under the name of statesmanship, that of the lesser, known as household *management*, to women. (Philo, *Spec. Laws* 3.169-175)

The church also used family terms such as "household of God," "brothers and sisters," "Father," "fellowship," and they met in homes. The church was structured like an extended family and spiritually adopted others into their congregations. The church focused on children and saw conversion as "joining God's family." The family became a lens for the community to see God as a Father. It was important, however, that this new family be respected and honored in the Roman Empire. Leaders had to be good family men.

Elders Reflect Christ's Nature in the Family

How men led and cared for their family was also an important characteristic for leadership in the church. The elder was to be the husband of one wife or, in Greek, "a one-woman man" (*mias gunakais andres*).[108] The elder was to be faithful to his wife and a compassionate husband. Since the rate of divorce and remarriage was high in the Roman world, Christian leaders were going to have to set some strong standards as family men.[109] There has been strong debate over whether this "one-woman man" means that an elder cannot be divorced or simply that an elder is to be a good husband. Others may question whether the elder has to be married at all.

The evidence is strong on all sides, but I feel that marriage is preferred. Yet I also feel that the term that Paul uses, "one woman man," is very ambiguous and has no parallel currently found in any other Greek writing. Our English translations are equally as ambiguous. It is possible that if Paul wanted to say that an elder could not be divorced, he would have simply said it. It is hard to know what Paul meant by this phrase. He is clear in other passages concerning divorce (1 Cor. 7:11, 27), but in the Pastorals he chooses a phrase that is not as clear to us today. It is my opinion that each church will have to wrestle with this term and seek God's guidance to do what is best for its members. I also believe that church leaders should respect that other leaders and churches will be willing to wrestle out this issue with an honest desire to see the truth and be led by God's Spirit. I do believe, however, that husband-wife teams are best at fulfilling a shepherding ministry, and I hold to the view that Paul did have in mind elders being married. We find no record in the New Testament of single men being selected as elders, although we have evidence that Paul and Timothy, as single men, were evangelists. I do acknowledge that I have to remain open concerning the interpretation of this text.

Whatever side of the discussion one chooses we can agree that Paul is saying something about the elder's relationship with his wife. In the Greco-Roman world, husbands typically had courtesans for their public encounters while their wives stayed at home and managed the family or delegated this responsibility to slaves. At Crete, women were trained for one to two years to manage the family before they married.[110] Afterward they took over the house. This created an emotional distance between husbands and wives. When Paul encourages women to submit to their husbands by respecting and supporting them, he was telling them to continue to do what they had been doing socially (Eph. 5:22-24). But when Paul told husbands to submit to their wives by loving and nurturing them sacrificially, he was calling them to go against their culture (Eph. 5:21, 25-33; Col. 3:19).

For Paul, an elder candidate was one who was in love with his wife and was not the typical husband in the Roman Empire. "One-woman man" *at least* means that elders are good, faithful, loving, and compassionate husbands. Whatever we decide about the translation of "one-woman man," we can all agree that Paul expected the elder to be a good, sexually and emotionally faithful, loving husband. They are expected to be devoted husbands to the one they are currently married. Men who are distant, controlling, and/or poor models of Christian husbands *should never become elders unless they repent, work through this sin, and change their behavior.*

Paul also challenged elders to be good fathers. In the early church, elders were appointed to lead the Christian community (Acts 14:23). In addition to having personal and moral qualities, these elders were expected to be family men. They were also expected to "lead" (*prohistemi*) their household in order to effectively *prohistemi* the church. Traditionally, this word has been translated "manage" or "rule," suggesting control over the family (1 Tim. 3:8).[111] The quotes at the beginning of this chapter illustrate that *management* was an important quality for a successful father/husband even though his wife or a hired slave actually did the hands on work.[112] The word suggests control as with a steward or slave in charge of keeping financial account. Paul uses a different word even though it has been translated *manage*. *Manage* may not be a good term to use. Managing (*oikonomos*) was a common practice for fathering in a home, however Jesus charged the disciples not rule over each other (Mk. 10:41-45). The women or slave who managed in the home were seen as people with low honor.[113] Not only was the concept foreign to Jesus' call to fathers, the word that Paul uses for a father's involvement in the home was different than *management* (*oikonomos*).

A closer look at *prohistemi* suggests involvement rather than control or management. This translation of the word proposes that the early Christian elders did not delegate their children to slaves nor neglect their homes, but they took part in the affairs of their families. This could be accomplished directly through serving, teaching, nurturing, and maintaining personal contact with their wives, children, and slaves (Eph. 5:25-6:9).

Prohistemi in Greek Literature

Prohistemi is used in Paul's letters eight times. In the Pastorals (1, 2 Timothy and Titus) *prohistemi* is used in reference to doing good works (Tit. 3:8, 14), serving as an elder (1 Tim. 5:17), and involvement of the elders and deacons with children, household, or church (1 Tim. 3:4, 5, 12).[114] Traditionally, *prohistemi* has been translated to manage or rule, but does this word indicate control or involvement? In Paul's letters to the churches, this word was used in two texts. In Rom. 12:8 "the *one leading* [or being active] does it in eagerness," and in 1 Thess. 5:12 "those who labor with you and *lead you* in the Lord and warn you . . ." are leaders worthy of respect. They are Christians who work with, labor for, and encourage/warn the congregation. In these texts, *prohistemi* indicates leadership or active work rather than management.

In the Greek Old Testament, this word was used for Hebrew words which also suggest involvement or an inner room of a home (Is. 43:24; 2 Sam. 13:17; Amos 6:10; and Prov. 23:5, 26:17). It is also used in 1 Macc. 5:19 for leading or standing before the people. In the Greek Old Testament, *prohistemi* indicates involvement, activity, or leadership that is central to the home or community. It does not suggest management or control. In other Greek writings, the word meant leadership, going in front of the community, protecting the poor, and serving as an ambassador.

Elders and *Prohistemi*

Since *prohistemi* indicates involvement or active leadership, the elders were to be active leaders in their homes. Elders were also to display this type of involvement in the church (1 Tim. 3:5, 5:17). First, this means that the elders were active family men who played an important role in training and developing their children. While this intimacy within their families may have been counter cultural, they modeled God's love with the creation. Because of their involvement their children were submissive, reflecting respect for their father.

Second, this word suggests that the elders and deacons did not neglect their children and spouses. The family played an important role in their lives. Since upper-class Roman males delegated much of the child rearing to slaves or other family members, it is possible that Paul is suggesting that elders be those who were involved in rearing their own children (Eph. 6:4; Col. 3:21). Elders were fathers who took an active role in parenting and guiding their children. Yet this was a counter cultural method for parenting at the time of Paul.

Prohistemi in the Context of the Roman Fathers (*Paterfamilias*)

In Roman families, fathers had complete power over their children, and this has led interpreters to view the father as harsh and cruel.[115]

On the whole, the young child seems to have been of minor interest
to the Roman literary classes. Childhood is occasionally invoked in a
detached and general way by adult authors as a symbol of the uned-
ucated or innocent human, but literary references to children and
childhood are relatively few and often vague, revealing little interest
in the activities of young children for their own sake.

It could be the oddities of survival that leave the modern reader with
the impression that Roman parents and Roman society were more
concerned with the moral and practical training of children than in
their cognitive, physical, and emotional development, but the surviv-
ing literature does support the conclusion that educators and medi-
cal writers were not as interested in the young child as their modern
equivalents are.[116]Pamper a child and he will terrorize you, play with
him and he will grieve you. Do not laugh with him or you will have
sorrow with him, and in the end you will gnash your teeth. Give him
no freedom in his youth and do not ignore his errors. Bow down his
neck in his youth and beat his sides while he is young or else he will
become stubborn and disobey you, and you will have sorrow of soul
from him. Discipline your son and make his yoke heavy so that you
may not be offended by his shamelessness.[117]

Children were instructed by slaves, called *pedagogues*, who tended to be
tough, and much of the development of children was left to babysitters, nurses,
and other slaves.[118] Evidence from inscriptions indicates that a strong bond,
lasting into adulthood, existed between these care givers and the children.[119]
It seems that in upper-class families fathers played more of a delegating role,
entrusting the major tasks of child development to slaves, schools, and wives.[120]
Women became supervisors of their households and tolerated their husband's
sexual affairs.[121] The wife was to be submissive and accept her husband's gods
and lifestyle. She was not to shame her husband or her family by resisting her
role in the family. Children were also expected to uphold the father's honor by
submission, respect, and public honor.[122] Fathers may have been strict, but they

were preparing their children to carry the honor of the family as well as the state. The Greco-Roman family was culturally and socio-economically driven. The father was concerned with politics in his home and the city. [123]

Christian parenting, however, involved compassion (Luke 11:1-12) and gentleness (Col. 3:21). Fathers rather than *pedagogues* were to discipline and instruct their children. Fathers were also challenged to train their children by *nurturing them in the instruction and warning of the Lord* as part of the Christian household rather than delegating this responsibility to child-minders and wet nurses (Eph. 6:4). This relational style of parenting would have been common of lower-class families, but not for the Hellenized upper-class families.

The father of the home/family was able to exercise *patria potestas* (father's power). The father was expected to exercise this power over the family, and the family in turn honored him through submission. In Roman culture, the father had almost unlimited power over the children concerning marriage, occupation, and childhood training. Controlling the family was a sign of strength, honor, and power wielded by father. Fathers were expected to dominate their children and home while their household showed respect through their obedience to them.

Elders and Christian Leadership in the Church

For many Roman families, parenting was about delegation and management. Jesus said that Gentiles rule over and exercise authority over one another (Mark 10:42). These terms indicate management and control (*oikomenos*), but Jesus indicated that this style of leadership was not part of the Christian way of life. Elders were charged not to lord or rule but to become examples to the flock (1 Peter 5:3). This Christian method of leadership was about service, not control. As elders shepherd (pastor) and give attention (bishop) to the congregation (Acts 20:28; 1 Peter 5:1-4), they practice a method of leadership that may be different than their culture. Their leadership involves looking to the interests of others (Phil. 2:1-4), [124] becoming examples to their families and community, protecting and serving the congregation and family (Acts 20:28, 35), and being involved in their families and churches (1 Tim. 3:4-5). Christian elders were charged to model service by practicing leadership in the home rather than control. They were to set an example for the congregation rather than manage or rule. Their leadership was not harsh, because harshness would create bitterness in those close to them.

The Pastoral Epistles suggest that elders be men who are involved in the affairs of their homes. They are not distant from their wives or their children. This is also a requirement for an elder to effectively lead a congregation. This is in conflict with the Roman view of control, management, or delegation from the father. This also contrasts with current translations of this word as "manage" or "rule." Elders and deacons were to be family oriented and involved with children, spouses, and house slaves. While the Romans used family management as a reflection of the state government, Christianity used family involvement as a reflection of church leadership. This application leaves us with the understanding that Christian leadership in the church and family is about involvement rather than control. Christian leadership must begin with this involvement and service in the home before it can be extended to the congregation.

CONCLUSION

Elders are men who lead incarnationally by modeling God's and Christ's character in the home. Since the church exists in a world that is many times resistant to God's will, elders help the church reflect the Creator's character and glory. Elders lead by setting an example for the flock (1 Peter 5). Elders are men who are blameless. This means that their character upholds the standards and teachings of Christ's church. While this may seem to be requiring elders to be perfect, blameless indicates that elders uphold God's standards. God wants people to become spiritually mature, compassionate, righteous, and faithful. The fruits of the Spirit are manifestations of God's nature. Elders are men who manifest God's character.

Elders do this by first being moral examples to their families, congregations, and community. This morality includes compassion, empathy, and peacefulness. In the Greco-Roman, culture this meant that the elders were to lead the congregation by living as God called his people to live. Elders were to be self-controlled, gentle, sober, and sexually pure with their wives. Elders do not have a different standard of conduct than other members of the church; they only prove that they can live by the ethical standards that God has given to his people.

Elders also are to be good family men. Paul wrote that the elder needed to be a man who was involved in his family. The word *prohistemi* suggests leadership by involvement, protection, and/or persuasion. The elder was a man who was involved with his family, which illustrated his ability to be involved with and lead a congregation.

Elders today need to model family values as well as compassion. Rather than finding men who can set visions and create dynamic plans for the congregation, churches need to seek men who can follow God's vision and plan in their families and for the flock. Men who are distant from and uninvolved with their families will be distant from and uninvolved in the church. Men who are harsh with their children will be harsh with other leaders, especially those who are younger. Men who are harsh with their wives will not be respected by the women in the church and community. They will be ineffective shepherds in modeling Jesus to others. With the high rate of abuse, divorce, and dysfunction in American families, Christians, and others need to see healthy families in the church.

Leaders who are dysfunctional in their family relationships will not be able to lead other generations to spiritual wholeness. They will not attract those seeking to become healthy. We must help families inside and outside the church heal, but this must come from incarnational leaders who model God's style of marriage and parenting. God has set the pattern; leaders follow and call others to do the same. They follow by modeling his nature through the fruits of the Holy Spirit, becoming a father like God, and being approachable. These individuals reflect God's character to both the church and the world.

Questions _____

1. Do you agree with the argument concerning managing family or involvement? Why or why not?

2. How were Christian fathers to be different than men/fathers in Roman societies?

3. What strengths can you find in yourself after reading this section?

4. What areas do you need to address in your life?

5. Would these be the same strengths and weaknesses that your wife and children attribute to you?

6. What is your course of action as a result of reading this chapter?

Chapter 7

ELDERS REFLECT THE NATURE OF CHRIST

In Chapters 5 and 6, I suggested that elders have two major characteristics. First, elders are spiritually mature and reflect the fruits of the Holy Spirit. Second, elders are great family men. These qualities were necessary for the first century church to reach into their communities and transform lives. These qualities are still necessary for elders to minister even today. In a world seeking Jesus, the church must seek the lost and model Jesus' nature in the community of faith. The church of the future, as well as today, needs moral guidance from leaders and will respect only those who model a mature spirituality.

This theme is clear in the Pastoral Epistles. In order to spread the gospel, Paul is concerned that the church model holiness in three areas. First, Paul wanted the church to *stress healthy morality*. Musonius Rufus was a Roman philosopher who wrote near the time of Paul. Rufus uses the term "healthy teaching" (*hygia disdaskalia*) quite often in his writing, and he relates it to educational instruction, character, and philosophy (*Discourse* 1:10). Paul also uses this term in reference to morals (1 Tim. 1:11; Titus 2:1). In all of these passages healthy teaching is a statement about moral actions.

We also know that the law is made not for the righteous but for those who break the law, rebels, ungodly, sinful, unholy, irreligious, those who murder their fathers and mothers, adulterers, perverted, slave traders, liars, perjurers, and *whatever else is against healthy teaching* (sound doctrine). (1 Tim. 1:9-11)

In the Restoration Movement, we have tended to use this phrase (translated sound doctrine) in reference to church doctrine. Yet Paul uses this word for morality. He suggested that morals are a key element in the church's outreach to the world. Elders were to teach these morals (Titus 1:10), and Titus was called to rebuke elders and members not practicing these morals (Titus 1:13). The Jewish troublemakers at Crete were condemning the Cretans for their morality (1:12). Paul acknowledged that the Cretans were immoral (1:12) and called Titus to empower the elders to have a character that would be irrefutable by these false teachers (1:14). Sound doctrine is morality.

Second, the church was to model a *good conscience*. Paul wanted the church to have this good conscience (1 Tim. 1:5; 3:9; 4:2), which was the result of a pure heart, sincere faith, and love. The leaders (deacons) were to hold the faith with a good conscience (1 Tim. 3:9). This is why leaders needed to be blameless, good family men, and spiritually mature. Paul wanted the churches at Ephesus and Crete to glorify God with their moral conduct (Titus 2:11-13).

Finally, Paul wanted the church to *live in peace*. The early Christians were under suspicion by the Roman Empire of practicing an illegal religion. Morality and insurrection were two major accusations leveled against illegal religions in the Empire. Paul called the churches to live in peace and harmony by praying for and obeying authorities (1 Tim. 2:1-4) and by doing good deeds (1 Tim. 5:24; Titus 2:14; 3:8, 14).

Elders were to be peaceful men who had a good reputation with outsiders. If the church was going to survive in a hostile culture, God's leaders needed to model peace, morality, and be family men. Elders not only helped the church mature and practice healthy morals, have a good conscience, and, live in peace; they modeled these qualities.

Christ is the incarnation of God. This incarnation was relational, descending to the earth among men (Eph. 4:7-10), and organizational, the distribution of leadership gifts according to God's grace (4:11-13). Leadership is a gift as is salvation (2:6-8). The gifts of apostles, prophets, evangelists, shepherds, and teachers are for the church.[125] Christ left elders and other leaders behind so that they might reflect his leadership and guide the church to follow him. Unity is a reflection of the reconciliation, forgiveness, mercy, and compassion of Christ.[126] Jesus died to reconcile all people (2:11-15) to God and one another.[127] Jesus gave leaders to the church, who would then also model this life of reconciliation and unity. According to Paul, Christian elders are those who work with evangelists, teachers, and other leaders to continue the task of Christ to promote unity and help the body grow. They do this by imitating Jesus.

They do this by living incarnational lives themselves and leading the church to live incarnational lives.

Elders Help the Church Become Like Christ

The text does not suggest a hierarchy. While elders shepherd the church, each leader has their giftedness/role in leading God's people. Elders, ministers, teachers, deacons, and other leaders work *together* to build up the body. Paul told the church that the purpose of leaders was to restore God's people as a healthy body. The word *kartizo* means to complete, put into proper condition, prepare, create, mend, or bring together.[128] Paul told the church that Jesus united, saved, reconciled, and accepted sinful people. Leaders are expected to do the same. Elders and their wives have the responsibility to help renew the church so that the congregation may follow Christ. The church follows Christ in three areas (Eph. 4:11-16).

Into the work of ministry

First, the church practices service/ministry (*diakonos*, Eph. 4:12). Some translations use ministry or service for *diakonos*.[129] The word can also mean a broker, administrator, or "go-between." The *diakonos* helps or empowers someone. Ministry in the Greco-Roman context suggests empowering others to be what they need to be. This is done through service, encouragement, and work, but it is not limited to service. Elders help the church practice this ministry in the world.[130]

Christ practiced *diakonos*. Jesus came to *minister* (*diakonos*), not to have others *minister* to him (Mark 10:43). Paul was made a *diakonos* because of the mystery of God's will (Eph. 3:7). The church is to carry that ministry into the world and call people out of darkness to God. This not only involves service, but it also suggests guidance, proclamation, mediation, and empowerment.

To build up/encourage the body of Christ

Next, the church encourages itself (Eph. 4:12). The church is to build members up for unity in the faith.[131] The church is to carry on the work of Christ in peace, unity, and reconciliation. Elders and other leaders help the church work out their problems and maintain peace and harmony. They practice reconciliation so that the congregation can preserve the shared bond of peace (Eph. 4:3). When the church is united, it becomes a place where Christians can grow in their faith and develop their spirituality without fear or rejection.

Jesus brought the Jews and Gentiles together in order to unite them into God's holy family so that they may be knit together and grow into a temple (Eph. 2:19). The Spirit dwelt among them as they were built together (Eph. 2:21-22). Jesus united people in order to build each other up, so that there would be growth and unity. This unity came at the cost of Jesus' blood (Eph. 2:13). Elders and leaders continue this practice of reconciliation and unity in the body as a reflection of Christ to the community of faith.

To a mature human, to the measure of the fullness of Christ

When the church practices ministry and edification, it matures and grows. Usually we think of this word as perfect (which is how it is translated at times). *Telos* does not mean perfect, but complete or mature.[132] Jesus calls the Christian to be mature, as the Father is mature (Matt. 5:43-48). Paul encouraged the church to pursue love, which brings maturity (1 Cor. 13:8). *Telos* is not perfection (which to many is an unattainable state) but maturity.[133] This is the goal of Christians. The church also grows to completion, which means that it matures and develops as it should. The goal is not perfection but maturity. Elders and their wives help Christians grow and mature so they will not be deceived by false teachers and fall from grace (Eph. 4:14).

> Many take Christ's words and apply them backwards. They teach that if you have position in the Kingdom of God it is important to lead as a servant. But Jesus meant us to see that those who first serve are indeed the leaders that others will follow. Position and title are useless in such a scenario. Jesus, of course, is our prime example. He did not have any title or position in this world, yet He spoke with authority unlike any man who ever walked the earth.[134]

Jesus calls Christians to maturity (Matt. 5:43-48; Luke 8:1-6). Jesus helps Christians mature by teaching them God's Word. He also models God's leadership style and nature. Christians are to develop and mature in the image of God through Jesus. Elders and their wives carry on the work of helping the body mature and grow in a relationship with Jesus. They involved in the spiritual development of God's people. They do this by empowering the church to practice ministry and edification.

The goal of this maturity and edification is unity of the faith, knowledge of Jesus, love, and a resistance to heresies. The church is to grow and develop in order that Christians may be equipped to go into the world, resist sin, and proclaim the gospel of Christ. We have learned from this discussion of Eph. 4:12-16 that leaders, including elders, help the church become mature as they practice ministry and encourage the church to be united and continue the work of Jesus.

Maturity is manifested when a person is able to love and forgive. Jesus tells us that God is mature because God loves enemies (Matt. 5:48). Paul calls love, "that which is mature/complete," (1 Cor. 13:8).[135] In 1 Cor. 14, Paul instructs the church to mature by seeking and practicing *agape* love. This is done by prophecy rather than tongues (which is self-centered). It is a desire to build up others. Love is the fruit of maturity.

People look for leaders that build teamwork. These leaders work with people to develop their talents and gifts to their full potential. This team concept seems to fit Paul's model of leadership in the church. Leaders do not create a new vision; they help the church attain the vision that God has set before them. Elders and their wives lead the way by modeling Christ's work for the church. They then help the church imitate Christ's work by developing and persuading others to follow Christ's direction. In Heb. 13:17, Christians are told to be persuaded by their leaders (notice *peitho* does not mean obey but persuaded).[136] Peter told the elders to serve as examples for the flock (1 Peter 5:4). Paul also told the elders to watch the flock and shepherd them (Acts 20:28). Elders are given the task of carrying on the work of Christ with Christians.

In Bruce Tulgan's book, *It's OK to Be the Boss*, he suggests that management is less about control and more about hands on work with employees.[137] His book addresses the dilemma that many companies face with the rising Millenial/Buster/Generation X generation in the workforce and the conflict that Baby Boomer employers find with these workers. Tulgan, a member of this generation, indicates that empowerment does not mean leaving the employee to themselves and hoping they will become productive. He suggests that empowerment means being involved in the lives of these workers and finding creative ways to motivate them to be the best they can be and to help the company succeed. Management is not always about control. Empowerment does not always mean we relinquish control. Management and empowerment suggest that leaders become involved with others and guide them to develop. It also suggests that leaders communicate vision and goals to those they work with, so that both can bring out the best in each other and the team.

Conclusion

Elders do not create a vision for the church; they follow the vision that Christ has given his church. They work with other leaders according to their giftedness to build up the body of Christ and mature the members. Jesus practiced reconciliation in order that his people might have access to God, unity, encouragement, and peace. He accomplished this in the incarnation through his death on the cross. This death brought salvation to all so that Jews and Gentiles could be united. This mystery was proclaimed to the world and shown through the church, which displays the multifaceted wisdom of God (Eph. 3:10).

Jesus gave leadership as a gift to the church so that it might continue to grow and be united. Elders, along with ministers, teachers, and missionaries, are part of the process that Christ has for His people. Elders and their wives imitate Christ by practicing unity, reconciliation, and mercy within the body of Christ. They do this so that the church can develop spiritually and grow to maturity. They lead organizationally by making sure that members grow and mature in their faith. They are attentive to those who are in danger of being deceived by sin (Eph. 4:14) or causing conflict within the church.

QUESTIONS

1. What ethical issues does Paul think are important for leaders and the church to practice in society?

2. What has been our traditional definition of "sound doctrine?" How do you feel about this now?

3. How do we practice healthy teaching in the 21st Century church?

4. How is this important for evangelism?

5. What are some of the strengths you see in yourselves after reading this chapter?

6. What are some of the weaknesses you can identify in yourself?

7. What will be your course of action?

Chapter 8

SHEPHERDING FOR EVANGELISM THROUGH DISCIPLESHIP

I n the first section of this book, I made a case for elder development. Churches and ministers need shepherds so that all in the body of Christ can grow. In the second section, I suggested that elders can model God's style of leadership, which is manifested in Jesus and the Spirit. This leadership is *incarnational leadership*. Most importantly, elders must model the moral qualities of Jesus both in their families and in their witness for Christ. Elders and their wives who lead incarnationally serve among the people. This third section discusses issues that shepherds will face in modern congregations.

As mentioned in previous chapters, elder development is not only necessary for the spiritual development of the church, it is necessary for the evangelism of the church. In Acts 14 Paul and Barnabas appointed elders in newer congregations. This suggests that elders were important in helping the church continue the work of ministry and growth in the Kingdom. Paul's concern that Titus train and appoint elders was also an indication that elders are key to church development.

How are elders important to the growth and development of the church? I believe that elders help the congregation to grow by encouraging other leaders to use their giftedness in the body of Christ and by guiding the members to spiritual growth and health. Too often evangelism is viewed as one person's job. We hire ministers to preach and call us to evangelism. Yet, when we stop growing, the evangelist is the person we question the most. How many Bible studies are they doing? How many contacts are they making? How much time is being spent on sermon preparation, and how much time is spent knocking on doors?

While I agree that we as ministers need to set an example for the congregation, I believe that the task of evangelism does not rest solely on us. While I do believe that we need to set the pace in community involvement, outreach, and studies with others, the church grows when the members "preach the word wherever they go" (Acts 8:4). I also find that the current literature on church growth does not suggest that churches grow "if their ministers increase their number of Bible studies with the lost." Church growth literature suggests that churches grow when members invite, bring, and lead their friends and neighbors to the church. Growing churches are inviting outsiders into their communities and then leading them to conversion to Christ.[138] Preaching along with outreach ministries can help guide people to conversion, but the members are the ones who bring friends to the faith community.

The Missional/Incarnational Church

Newer literature on church growth suggests that churches should go through a paradigm shift. In the past churches were "attractional." This means that we would ask, "What can we do to get people to come to church?" We would focus on Sunday morning worship, the singing/music, and making the Sunday experience seeker friendly. Now, the question has changed. Since people aren't coming we have to ask the question, "How do we go and get people." The emphasis has now shifted from attraction to mission. Hirsch suggests that the missional-incarnational model comes from Jesus, who was sent from God to get people.

> The Incarnation not only qualifies God's acts in the world but must also qualify ours. If God's central way of reaching his world was to

incarnate himself in Jesus, then our way of reaching the world should likewise be incarnational. To act incarnationally therefore will mean in part that in our mission to those outside of the faith we will need to exercise a genuine identification and affinity with those we are attempting to reach. At the very least, it will probably mean moving into common geography space and so set up a real and abiding presence among the group. But the basic motive of incarnational ministry is also revelatory—that they may come to know God through Jesus.[139]

This view, common in Emergent Christianity is beginning to take root in our vocabulary and ministries. Leadership, therefore, must also practice this missional-incarnational method, not simply because it's the latest method, but because incarnational mission is biblical and models what God has done through Jesus. As the church pursues people and calls them to the journey of discipleship, elders must begin to help them develop, along with the other members of the church. Faith development, conflict resolution, recovery groups, and marriage ministries become a point of contact for people in the community. While it is important that elder couples have strong spiritual and marital relationships, they must also be able to embrace and guide those who enter the journey from an unchurched background.

Elders and their wives have the awesome task of helping these visitors and new Christians walk with Jesus. They have the opportunity to guide members to greater spiritual development in Christ while extending that invitation to others around them. Elders who shepherd the flock can do so with a focus on evangelism. While the ministers have an *intentionality* about evangelism, elders can encourage everyone to make this *intentionality* a major part of their life. They can encourage the members to keep their hearts on evangelism while modeling this in their lives.

Believers who assert that the church is intended only for Christians assume continued preaching to believers will mature them to the point where they will evangelize the unchurched. I have yet to see this happen. Churches that are not *intentionally* evangelistic do not *become* evangelistic through quality Bible teaching *alone*. When the church exists for feeding believers only, those believers become spiritual sponges that absorb more and more knowledge. If those sponges do nothing but soak in a pool of their own learning, they eventually sour. An unchurched person can hardly feel welcome in such a setting.[140]

Elders and their wives can guide the church to see evangelism as everyone's responsibility, not just the preacher's and model this in their lives and ministries. They can encourage the church to continue in discipleship.

DISCIPLESHIP JESUS' WAY

Discipleship is an interesting word. It has been discussed quite often in churches. It is a concept that has been abused, refused, and misconstrued. One of the basic studies that I remember receiving when I was converted was about discipleship. I remember that this study was the first time that I had really come face-to-face with this term. Since my conversion, I have noticed that discipleship is a common term in many churches. People mean different things by the term. I sometimes think that it has lost its original meaning in the way we use the term. Yet it is an ancient term that suggests deep concepts, relationships, and goals for those seeking to be disciples of Jesus.

The Greek word for disciple is from the word for learner (*manthano*). Similar terms were used in the Egyptian, Assyrian, Babylonian, Sumerian, and Jewish literature for a teacher and his many students (*lmd, edubba, ummia*).[141] Education was highly valued in these cultures, and a skilled teacher might be financially supported by his students/learners. *Manthano* was a popular word in the early Greek period, but the word began to fade out of the literature by the second century BC.[142] During Jesus' and Paul's time on earth, *manthano* once again became a common term in Greek and Roman literature. While Jesus walked this earth, the term became popular and the student/teacher relationship was revived.

It's not surprising that Jesus would use this term to relate Jewish concepts of covenant, devotion, cleaving, and submission in the Greco-Roman world

(Paul did the same thing with the word for reconciliation). Yet, the word for disciple carried some important understandings to the first-century listener.

The Structure of Discipleship

First, discipleship involved a *relationship* between student and teacher. This relationship suggested a structure and *relationship of authority*. The boundaries were clear, and the relationship was mutual, but not equal. The teacher had the authority to command, teach, convey information, and expect payment/submission from the student. If the student (or their parent) chose this relationship, they agreed to follow the teacher. *They always had the option to leave, stop payment, or walk away.* Sometimes a friendship existed but it developed after the student matured and later became a teacher.

The ancient world had different *types of relationship*. The chart below shows these two categories and different types under each. These relationships were *kinship/friendship* and *authority/discipleship*. One type was *authority relationships*. These relationships involved business contacts, patron/client, teacher/disciple, master/slave, and ruler/subjects relationships. These relationships did not promote equality; they assumed a structure of authority and submission. The boundaries were clear, and those who were clients, disciples, slaves, or subjects knew that those above them were in authority. The relationships existed by payment, debt, or conquest, but they required submission (willing or unwilling) by the lesser in the relationship. The one in authority always had the potential to abuse the lesser. That is why there are many Greek and Roman texts that give guidelines to patrons and teachers/philosophers concerning mercy, compassion, and ethical treatment of others.[143] Those in authority were warned about abusing others, but it sometimes still happened.

> The kings of the Gentiles lord it over them; and those who exercise authority over them call themselves benefactors [patrons]. You are not to be like that. Instead the greatest among you should be like the youngest, and the one who rules like the one who serves . . . I am among you as one who serves. (Luke 22:25-28)

Another type was *kinship relationships*. These involved family, extended family, personal friends, and those taken into one's home. These relationships existed through love, devotion, blood, and marriage. They consisted of a close circle of people who were related and accepted each other. While the patriarch was the head of the family, there was an atmosphere of equality and intimacy that existed in these relationships.

Kinship	Authority
Family	Patron/Client
Friends	Master/Slave
Adopted	Teacher/Disciple
Widowed	Ruler/Subjects
Strangers	Leader/Follower
Hired Hands	

Figure 6: Relationships in the Ancient World

Second, *discipleship involved persuasion*. Musonius Rufus (a Roman philosopher at the time of Paul) wrote that an effective teacher used proofs/examples *to persuade his students to learn*.[144] In 2 Cor. 5:9, Paul wrote that the job of the church was to persuade people. Aristotle indicated that a speaker's/teacher's effectiveness was seen by their argument, passion, and character (*logos, pathos, ethos*).[145] A good teacher was not one who used power and authority over the students. The good teacher persuaded the students by their life, passion, and truth of a doctrine. Effective teachers do not force disciples, but they encourage and empower them to choose what is best. The translation of Heb. 13:17 is not submit to the leader's authority but to be persuaded (*peitho*) by their authority. The word for obey is the word "listen." The life and faith of the leaders are to be an example for the Christians. Disciples were never called to blindly trust and follow their teachers. The teachers had the responsibility to be good, compassionate, ethical, and effective teachers/leaders for the church.

Third, *discipleship involved being part of a group*. The teacher had disciples (plural). In most cases the successful teachers were careful not to focus on one student. Since they made their living teaching. They were also judged by the number of disciples that they had. In John 6:66, Jesus' reputation (according to the culture) as a teacher was at risk when many of the disciples left. The remaining 12 showed others that he was still a valuable teacher. Eastern culture is group oriented (as opposed to Western culture, which is individualistic). The teacher in the ancient world and Bible times created a learning environment with a group of students. Discipleship/teaching was not one-on-one because teachers needed many pupils, both financially and for honor. In the case of Seneca and Nero, the teacher had a single student but this only reflected the fact that the Emperor Claudius and his wife had the money to hire Seneca just for their son. Those in the first century understood the structure and nature of discipleship. The relationship conveyed a sense of authority and submission and the expectation of a group being trained by the teacher/discipler. There was always the potential for the person in authority to be abusive. There was always the potential for the teacher to cheat the students. Yet Jesus and the church, like many ancient writers, challenged those in leadership positions to serve, empower, and lead with mercy and grace.

While we do not see single disciple-student relationships in the Bible, we know that Jesus had disciples, Paul had a mission team, and the early church practiced discipleship with leaders and members. In Eph. 4:11-16, elders, teachers, apostles, evangelists, and prophets help the members mature and grow in the faith. Discipleship can exist when leaders train, develop, teach, and guide Christians to learn and grow in Jesus. Disciples need to be part of a community where they can grow, develop, and work with leaders to be the best they can be.

How is Discipleship Practiced?

Discipleship has been used by churches over the centuries. Campus ministries and para-church organizations since the 1960s have been criticized for using and/or abusing this relationship. Growth happened with discipleship but abuse within these organizations has also been a concern of those studying movements. In the mainline Churches of Christ, we have not been as effective in evangelism nor in keeping our members in the faith so that they might grow. We have not provided accountability for our members who struggle in sin. International Churches of Christ have also struggled over discipleship issues. We both need to ask the question, "How can we practice discipleship Jesus' way?"

First, *those who have biblical authority can and should disciple others.* Our leaders need to see their role as discipling the whole congregation, groups in the congregation, and those training for leadership roles. Discipleship was rarely one-on-one. Discipleship existed in a relationship where the teacher led a group. While this relationship may be misused, the value of a group of disciples is that they can hold the leader accountable (with their feet; they can leave an abusive leader). Other leaders within the congregation can also hold each other accountable. Discipleship is biblical, but it carries a sense of authority. Jesus' way of discipleship involves respect, persuasion, empowerment, guidance, service, and mercy in leadership.

Elders carry the responsibility of being like Christ by discipling with integrity. They must effectively guide and persuade the congregation by their character, passion, and devotion to Jesus and others. The responsibility rests on them to provide a healthy, safe, trusting, and secure environment for the disciples to grow and develop. They use compassion and empathy to disciple others.

One-on-one discipleship can deviate from the understanding of discipling. It is less common than group discipling in the Bible and ancient world. Groups provide accountability. Misuses of discipleship have happened when those without authority from God disciple or when a leader enters into a discipling relationship with one person.

Plans fail for lack of counsel, but with many advisers they succeed
(Prov. 15:22)
For waging war you need guidance and for victory many advisers.
(Prov. 24:6)

The biblical "one another" or "each other" passages are written to the community as a whole. The texts can simply be translated "love others" or "bear with others," (suggesting not just those in the church but those outside—John 13:34-35) or as we would say down south, "all y'all" or "you all." The idea of confessing sins "to others" or "to each other" (James 5:16) refers to group accountability in the context of elders praying for those spiritually and physically sick. Abuses of discipleship happen most often when groups practice one-on-one discipling. The one-on-one or one-to-one discipling relationships may place the "discipler" in a position of authority that God usually has not supported.

The Pastorals are an example of this group discipleship. The letter is not only Paul's discipling of Timothy or Titus, it was Paul's way of discipling the many members of his mission team as well as other churches. Paul's writings are written to groups that are his way of discipling many individuals at the same time. The Pastoral letters are also a statement to the Ephesian and Cretan communities that these men (Timothy and Titus) were his successors and carried his authority.[146] These two men discipled the churches and leaders where they were sent to minister. The use of "steward/manage" that Paul used for their ministry also suggested that they were his servants/managers who carried his authority and will in their work as evangelists.[147]

Second, *we need to develop the kinship relationships in our churches.* The church spread throughout the world not just by "discipling relationships" but by family relationships.[148] The church was characterized by family terms such as "father," "brothers and sisters," "fellowship," "household," "stewards," "table fellowship," "friendship," "yokefellows," and "family" and by using homes for early worship and fellowship. These relationships were greatly missing in the first century, especially among slaves and foreigners. The call to abandon family for Jesus meant that the disciple needed a family. The disciple became part of an in-group or family and began to develop kinship relationships. These relationships were characterized by mutuality, equality, and love. They provided accountability, support, and trust. One-on-one or one-to-one relationships fall into this category.

In these relationships no one has authority, but intimacy exists when it is freely given by the disciple and is based on trust, time, and respect. No one can force this relationship or intimacy. The Bible does not force disciples into this type of accountability. It is developed through time and a sense of trust. People cannot be paired up or assigned this type of intimate relationship. They gravitate to those whom they respect and willingly begin the process of growth together. Phil 3:17 calls the church to seek relationship with mature

Christians who have Paul's view of the faith. These relationships are keeping people in small groups, the church, and the faith. Finally, *discipleship is a call to world evangelism*. In Matthew 28:19-20, Jesus says:

> *Go, disciple all nations/gentiles*, baptizing them in the name of the Father, Son, and Holy Spirit; teaching them all that I have commanded to you.

I have heard this passage commented on for years. Concerning discipleship, some have said that this passage teaches that you become a disciple, then get baptized, then continue to be taught. Some have supported infant baptism (baptize the baby, then teach). Others have said that evangelism (baptism) is different/separate from discipleship. The word for disciple (*manthano*) is a verb. The two verbs (participles) following disciple (baptize and teach) define or explain how to "disciple." The term for nations is also the term for Gentiles (imagine how the Jewish disciples and Matthew's Jewish readers would have heard and read this). The point I am making is that the church is called to disciple the world by baptizing and teaching others about Jesus. This means that the church carries the integrity, character, and passion of Jesus. It means that our leaders are not to lead with power and coercion, as do some in the world, but with love and persuasion.

Discipling involves baptism and teaching. Leaders guide people to salvation by developing relationships and showing them Jesus in their lives and teaching. Church leaders disciple non-Christians by introducing them to Jesus in baptism and then continuing to teach the church (and community) all the lifestyles of Jesus. Small groups, support/accountability groups, and educational classes are a tremendous opportunity for leaders and elders to shepherd and develop people in their community and church.

Conclusion

Discipleship is a word and relationship that first century readers recognized. It was a relationship that carried authority, respect, mercy, and integrity.

Leaders discipled people. Jesus' leaders persuaded others by their life, teaching, and character in the faith, not by force and coercion. They also discipled the world by proclaiming the gospel of Jesus and develop relationships with those outside of Christ. Those being discipled had a voice and a choice. Discipleship is desperately needed in churches. It begins with evangelists, elders, teachers, and other leaders modeling Jesus' style of leadership in their community.

Yet kinship also existed in the church. People developed personal relationships through trust, love, and openness. These relationships developed with time and patience.

They were not forced. As the family relationship grew, the disciple matured spiritually and emotionally. This also is desperately needed in our churches.

Elders have the responsibility to work with the other leaders and the church to develop these relationships. First, elders and other leaders, have the authority to disciple the congregation and those in the world to be closer to Jesus. Second, elders can help the church develop friendship/kinship relationships in the body through small groups, ministries, and intimate friendships. These two types of relationships will help members to develop spiritually and will help the church to envelop people outside of the body of Christ. They will also enable the church to continue to evangelize their world and communities for Jesus.

QUESTIONS _____

1. What are the two relationships that were important in the ancient world and are still important in the world today?

2. What is discipleship? How is it manifested in the church?

3. What is kinship? How is it manifested in the church?

4. How has discipleship been abused or misused?

5. How does discipleship fit into evangelism?

6. How can elders shepherd a church for evangelism?

7. What are some areas that you need to work on to be prepared to shepherd the church to growth?

8. What will be your course of action?

SECTION THREE

ISSUES FACING TODAY'S GOOD SHEPHERDS

Chapter 9

DEVELOPING FAITH IN THE MEMBERS

Discipleship was an important role in any community in the ancient world. Those living in that world received strength from their various communities. The biblical world was not individualistic. It was a world where people saw themselves as part of a community. An individual grew and was protected in communities such as families, clubs, associations, guilds (similar to our modern unions), and religious groups. All of these communities practiced acceptance, fellowship, and guidance.[149]

Teachers practiced discipleship among their groups of students. Much of the teaching involved reflection, discussion, and fellowship. The teachers modeled behavior through their actions, speeches, and interactions with students and or through their writings to an extended community.[150] The ancient world practiced community through group dynamics.

The church was born in this Eastern culture. The church understood the concepts of community, sharing, fellowship, and leadership (Acts 2:44-47; 4:34-37). Their leaders discipled members of their communities to maturity and ministry. The Hebrew writer suggests that the community was a place of security, support, and growth for the Christian.

> Let us hold firmly to the hope we profess, for the one who promised is faithful. Let us consider how to provoke others to love and good

works. Let us not give up gathering together [this is the word for synagogue] as some have the habit of doing. Let us encourage others even more as you see the day approaching. (Heb. 10:23-25)

Paul wrote to the Christians at Ephesus that leadership was a gift given to the church to help members mature in their faith.

To prepare God's people for ministry, so that the body of Christ may be encouraged until we all reach unity in the faith and in the knowledge of the Son of God and become mature . . . (Eph. 4:12-13)

Leaders, especially elders, have the responsibility to help members develop their faith and mature spiritually.

What Is Faith Development?

Faith development has been a discipline in religious/biblical studies for a few decades. Faith development has become an important issue in religious educational writings as well as in youth ministry and pastoral studies. First, the earliest scholar in this area was James Fowler. Fowler examined the human development processes described by human development scholars such as Piaget, Kohlberg, and Erickson and observed that faith, like human development, grew in stages.[151] Just as humans develop physically and emotionally through stages (beginning with birth), so we, as those created in the image of God develop our faith in stages.[152] Just as human developmental stages are necessary to the growth and maturity of all human beings, so must our faith develop in stages for our maturity and spiritual formation. Fowler listed seven stages of faith development from birth to retirement/old age. He believed that these seven stages of faith occurred through "transitions" in our spiritual experiences.

While the concept of faith development has been the basis of many publications concerning the development of Christians of all ages, it is also a concept being studied in the area of leadership. Ploch and Hastings indicate that children who stay faithful in their church membership and involvement (after leaving home) attribute their convictions to their parents' faith convictions.[153] The researchers initially studied more than 1,200 families attending church regularly and found that the children of parents who brought them to church claimed to be spiritual. Ploch and Hastings revisited many of the children years later, after they had left home. They found that some who attended regularly as children stopped attending after leaving home. Those who continued to attend claimed that their parents' convictions (called salience of faith by the writers) and practice of faith, rather than those just "taken to church," influenced them to continue after leaving home.

Kwilecki suggests that the development of personal religious belief development occurs best in churches/religions with leadership that has clear authority, revelation, and teachings concerning the Bible and the practice of faith.[154] Kwilecki believes that those churches in which leadership was not clearly defined or spiritual disciplines were not stressed had a more difficult time expressing their faith. Researchers at Biola University have also produced evidence that spiritual faculty members who mentor incoming freshman from nonreligious homes have a tremendous impact on their faith.[155] Upon graduation, these students had developed their faith to a level equal to or greater than their peers who came from religious homes. Christian leaders who mentor younger people clearly play an important role in faith development.

What can we learn from this?

- Faith can and must be developed in all humans, especially Christians.
- Times of intervention are needed for the individuals to grow beyond their personal boundaries and comfort zones.
- Faith development requires guidance and mentoring from spiritually mature people.
- Faith development is best achieved in a community.
- Spiritual disciplines can help faith grow and mature.
- The goal of faith development (spiritual maturity) is sacrificial love for the community, God, and others. Spiritual maturity is achieved when people love others unconditionally and practice acts of faith, charity, and service to others. God has called Christians to mature and be a people who love others and serve in our communities (Matt. 5:43-48; Titus 2:14; 3:8).

FAITH DEVELOPMENT AT CORINTH

The church at Corinth is a great example to use for faith development. While many of us see the Corinthian congregation as a place of ungodliness, sin, and rebellion, it helps to understand from where they had come. Corinth was a city that had worked hard to gain Roman approval and support. The city had been destroyed about 144 BC by Lysius Mumus and was rebuilt as a Roman city by Julius Caesar in 44 BC. The city was Roman in its customs and practices, but it still had a rich Greek history.

Because of this history the new Christians struggled with various background issues. The patron/client and disciple/student relationships resulted in a spirit of contention among the Corinthian people (1 Cor. 1-4).[156] The socioeconomic distinctions and honor/shame system of interaction in the city created divisions and tensions among the people.[157] The strong emphasis on idolatry, homosexuality, and prostitution in Corinth (as in any port city) also provided each male Christian the constant opportunity to leave the Christian faith and turn back to a life of sexual impurity (1 Cor. 6:12-20). The early church at Corinth struggled with many of these issues. In Paul's letter to this church, it is evident that the Christians battled to overcome sins such as allowing sexual sin and prostitution in the community (5; 6:12-20); social, economic, legal, and cultural animosity in the community worship and daily life (1-4; 6:1-8; 11:17-33); and idolatry (8:1-10).

According to Paul, much of this behavior stemmed from human wisdom (experience) being elevated over God's wisdom, or spiritual wisdom (1 Cor. 2:11; 8:2-3); jealousy and fighting (3:3; 5:8); pride and arrogance (4:18; 5:2); selfishness (9-10; 14); and humiliating the poor, slaves, and foreigners (6:7; 11:21-22, 33). The letter to this church is Paul's attempt to address these attitudes, which lead not only to sin but to division in the community of faith. Paul addresses these problems by calling the church to mature and develop their faith.

First, *Paul defined the problem*. Paul named their sins, attitudes, and behaviors and challenged them to live as people of the resurrection. Second, *Paul reminded them who they were*. Paul wrote that they were God's own possession (1 Cor. 3:16,23; 6:15,19; 7:23); reflections of Jesus (15:49); fully gifted by the

Holy Spirit (1:7; 2:12; 12:1-31); chosen and protected by God as weak people (1:27-28; 10:13); and in fellowship with Jesus as holy people (1:9; 6:9-11). By reminding them who they were, Paul created a distinction between their nature and their current actions. Their lifestyle was not a reflection of their divine calling, but their calling should have been reflected in their lifestyle.

Third, *Paul called them to maturity*. They had to mature and develop because their earthly, former, and worldly life was destined to pass away. The attitudes contrary to God were to pass away and be abolished (1 Cor. 1:29; 2:8, 14; 6:13). Human wisdom (and experiences) that were contrary to God's wisdom in the Spirit would be abolished. Because of this, they were to seek a more stable way of life, a life of love (*agape*). This love builds up (edifies, encourages) others and is greater than knowledge (8:2-3). It is the perfect/mature attitude and is permanent (13:8-13). It is the sign of maturity. When we love and give to others, we have grown and matured. We have put immature, temporary things behind. This causes us to see and know God, as Moses did, face to face (13:12; 8:3; Num. 12:8). This "face to face" with God is a sign that we have matured and are in intimate relationship with God. Love is the mature way, it calls us to grow up and put away childish, earthly things (1 Cor. 13:11). It is also the natural way. We are to naturally grow and mature and see God face to face. This has always been God's plan for us.

Finally, *this maturity/love was practiced in the context of community*. In 1 Cor. 8, acting from love caused the Gentile Christians (who see idols as dead images) to consider how and what they eat so that they do not offend the Jewish Christians, and weak Gentiles who struggled with idolatry. In 1 Cor. 9-10, love allowed the Christian to think of the benefit of others and be willing to make personal sacrifices. Love empowered the mature to build up (encourage, edify) other Christians through prophesying (speaking the word of God) or interpreting languages (12-14). Speaking in a language was only done to encourage others. The worship and community were not places for self-encouragement. The body of Christ should build *each other up* as Jesus and nurture his body through the Spirit and power of the resurrection. Paul believed that the body of Christ was mature when it practiced *agape* love for one another.

How Can Elders Develop the Faith of the Members?

Paul gave us an example of how to call a church to maturity. The church is mature when members practice *agape* love for one another. Members mature when they practice *agape* love from the heart for one another (especially those outside the faith community, Col. 3:14; 4:12; Matt. 5:43-48). Elders can shepherd the church by holding *agape* love as the standard in their lives and the congregation. In addition to *agape*, elders can cultivate an environment where all emotions and behaviors associated with *agape* (faith, hope, gentleness, self-control, encouragement, peace, compassion, empathy) are practiced and encouraged.

First, *elders can cultivate this environment by being people of agape.* This means that the elder has matured and regularly practices self-sacrificial love for his wife, family, small group, the church, and his neighbors. He (along with his wife) must model this form of love in all they do. Those inside and outside the church must see *agape* in them. Those who manifest *agape* are able to guide others to maturity because they are mature. Paul used himself as an example of this *agape* (1 Cor. 11:1). John tells us that God is agape (1 John 4:8). Jesus and God show us what maturity is to be. Maturity is a self sacrificing love for others. We cannot see God face to face until we mature through *agape*. Elders must be the example of spiritual maturity, compassion, and empathy and be a guide for others to grow and develop.

Second, *elders can shepherd other leaders in the church who also call the congregation to spiritual maturity* (Eph. 4:11-16). Too often leaders ask the question, "Who is in charge?" This is not a question for *agape* leadership. The question for *agape* leadership is, "How do we work together to help leaders manifest mature love?" Just as Jesus is the incarnation of God's love, so the church must reflect this love to the world. Therefore, leaders must reflect *agape* so that the church may grow. Elders must shepherd teachers to model *agape* and teach all ages to spiritually mature and develop. Elders must shepherd preachers to prophesy to the church and build up the body, and proclaim God's love to their communities. Sometimes the ministers have to call the church to holiness, outreach, and love. Elders must help ministers develop *agape* in their own lives and families and call the church to this love. Since elders model this love, they can call all leaders in the church (deacons, small group leaders, outreach leaders, worship leaders, ministry leaders, and others) to live *agape* in their families, communities, and the church.

Finally, *elders do not do this alone*. They work with other leaders to create a climate of *agape*. They not only pursue *agape* in their lives and relationships, they encourage it in others. They model and uphold the morals of compassion and empathy. They find opportunities for the members to connect with others in the body and grow in relationships and ministry. Elders work with ministers to develop a healthy congregation. Both leaderships can shepherd and work with those who are unchurched. Elders must also work with elders from other churches to learn from each other and discuss issues in their congregations which they may have in common.

Small groups help to foster intimate relationships within a larger church. Crisis counselors, support groups, and staff can help guide people through times of crisis and on to a more mature phase of life. Christian education programs can encourage members to mature through studying the Word of God and practicing *agape* within the body and surrounding community. Many times elders intervene in the lives of members to help them develop love and other associated attitudes. They intervene to help members heal, repent, forgive, and/or confront issues that hurt their emotional and spiritual growth. Other times elders empower others in the body to engage people and guide them to love and maturity. Faith development is a journey, and shepherds guide the sheep on the long journey to maturity.

Conclusion

Elders are called to develop their faith and reflect spiritual maturity. Faith development moves to *agape*. When the church practices this love, it grows both evangelistically and inwardly. This *agape* is the manifestation of God's love for us.

Agape is contagious. People want *agape*. *Agape* drives the church. *Agape* encourages empathy and compassion to grow and be manifested. *Agape* matures the church. *Agape* moves us into our community. *Agape* sends us overseas. *Agape* causes us to repent. *Agape* helps us to forgive. *Agape* affects all that we do. That is why Paul says it is the perfect/mature thing (1 Cor. 13:10). Paul also tells us that it is the fulfillment of the law (Rom. 13:10). Jesus calls it the greatest two commandments (Matt. 22:37-39). John tells us that this makes us complete/mature (1 John 4:12). God is *agape*, God is mature, and God is manifested in the love of Jesus. Yet, God is also to be manifested in us.

QUESTIONS

1. What is your definition of faith development?

2. How do people develop faith and grow in their faith?

3. What is the ultimate goal of faith development?

4. How is your *agape* being developed at this time?

5. How can elders help develop the faith of the congregation?

6. How is this important for evangelism?

7. What are some of the strengths you see in yourself after reading this chapter?

8. What are some of the weaknesses you can identify in yourself after reading this chapter?

9. What will be your course of action?

Chapter 10

Promoting Unity
in the Body of Christ

Unity is an important theme in the Christian faith. When we read Jesus' prayer, in John 17, we understand that he desired unity.

My prayer is not only for them. I pray also for those who will believe in me through their message, that all of them may be one, Father, just as you are in me and I am in you. May they also be in us so that the world may believe that you have sent me. (John 17:20-21)

This is a great prayer! Even during the stress of preparing for beating, crucifixion, and death, Jesus was thinking about his followers both present and future. Jesus' desire is that believers have the same unity that he and the Father share. Unity is one of our core values as a Christian community. Unity is necessary so that the world may believe that Jesus was sent by God the Father. Unity is a testimony to the deity and mission of Jesus Christ. The unity of believers is a testimony to the authenticity of our faith.

Unfortunately, Christian history shows, many times, that we have not emphasized unity. Sometimes we can't get along with our neighbors; other times we can't get along with each other. Christianity's "lack of unity" is one of the issues that drove Malcom X to join the Muslim faith. In the Restoration

Movement, we have also had our share of family feuds, a major plea has been
for harmony that calls all people everywhere to peace and unity in Jesus.

Over the years we have struggled to be an example of unity and harmony
in the world and among other churches in the United States.

I was traveling by airline from Chicago to Portland one summer. I had left
Tiranë, Albania, earlier that morning and was weary from the long European
leg of my trip home. On the airplane I sat next to an off-duty flight attendant
who also was traveling home. As we left Chicago, I began to talk with her. Susie
was from Korea, and I immediately mentioned that the largest church in the
world was in Seole. I asked if she had visited the church, and she told me she
was Buddhist. As the conversation progressed, she found out I was a minister and for the next thirty minutes she was quiet and did not initiate any further conversation. After an hour, I asked her about her faith. She was cold, but
finally, after my persistent questioning, she told me bluntly that she had no
room for Christians and the way "we" pressured others with our beliefs. She
also mentioned that we were divided, divisive, and rude.

Where does one go from this point? While I could have said that is not
how my "people act," the truth was that many times we have failed in our
example to those outside our faith communities. I said, "You're right." "We
have failed to make a good impression in this world. I feel like we screw up a
lot of people because of our own insecurities." She smiled but looked as if I
was setting her up for a "but we've all sinned . . ." statement. Next I said, "One
of the things I have appreciated about Buddhism is . . ." and mentioned a few
key points of her faith. From that point on we talked about the similarities
between Buddhism and Eastern Christianity (before the western worldview
dominated our history). The longer we talked, the more we found what we
had in common. As we landed she told me she had been overcritical of Christians and I must have a good church. She met my wife and boys and spoke to
them at the baggage terminal. She left smiling, while I left understanding how
unity works.

First, *unity finds common ground and works to build on that ground*. While
I am not Buddhist and I assume she has not converted to Christianity, we both

understood that what we had in common was worth discussing. On some things we thought alike. On other things we stood opposite. Yet, the focus on similarities draws people closer. It dissolves tensions. It opens the door for discussion. Unity builds relationships by seeking what we have in common.

Second, *unity exists under a vision or mission.* I have been involved with various domestic violence, abuse councils, and sexual assault teams in the Portland area. We provide trainings for ministers, police, and counselors from various agencies. I am the only member of the Churches of Christ/Christian Churches in these councils. In fact, I am sometimes the only one at some of these trainings/conferences who has a Christian worldview. If I focused on differences, I could argue about gender and sexual orientation issues, feminism, religions, legalization of narcotics, or the Iraq war. The sky would be the limit. Yet we have worked together well, provided many training workshops, and developed good relationships. How? We have a vision and a mission. Many have been in our home for dinner and some have come to church with us. Our goal is to get rid of abuse and violence in our world. We don't have time to argue. We know our work and that we have to work together. While we may have discussions about our differences and sometimes they can get a little heated, we understand that united we stand and divided we fall. I personally believe that Satan is enslaving our culture through abuse and trauma, and I know that I cannot fight this battle alone. I also know that when it comes to protecting victims, most of our differences are irrelevant.

Am I suggesting that we not take a stand for what we believe? Absolutely not! I am suggesting that we stop picking fights. I am suggesting that we stop avoiding people because they believe differently. I am suggesting that we become friends of others as Jesus did (Luke 5:30; 7:34). Should we be careful that we are not pulled into sin? Yes, but if we are that weak, it is our own fault. We should grow in our faith to be strong enough to live in the world and bless those who persecute us. We should be strong enough to be incarnated and not become carnal! We have lost our vision/purpose and we have spent years learning why everyone else is not like us. I am suggesting that this is why we devour even our own spiritual family.

Elders and Unity

Shepherds have an opportunity to promote unity and harmony in the body of Christ. Shepherds not only guide and protect the sheep, they help them stay together. Sheep scattered on the hillside (Ezek.34:5; Zech. 13:7; Matt. 26:31) was a negative metaphor. It was a picture that communicated fear, lack of vision, confusion, and death. The church needs to stand together and face Satan as one. We, like Jesus and the Father, must be united so that we can confront the spiritual forces of evil. Scattered sheep are easy prey. United sheep are hard to stop.

Yet, people have different interpretations of what unity means. For some, unity means that we all agree on something. This may be evident when there is disagreement on an issue, doctrine, or opinion. Those who display anxiety over not being supported, accepted, or agreed with usually feel that "thinking the same" is equal to unity. Sometimes leaders will not make a decision unless everyone is in agreement. At times issues are not resolved because leaders want to avoid conflict within the group so they choose to accept the will and direction of the few. In this situation, the few make the decision for the group because they will not support the majority. The remaining members agree to support the decision of the few and claim that this is unity. The few feel a calling to persuade the majority to come around to their opinion, which they believe is the truth (since only a *few* can be saved, Matt. 7:14). While this may result in a united decision, it is not unity. *Twelve Angry Men* was only a movie. It should not be a pattern for unity and solving an issue.

For others, unity means forcing the minority to go along with the majority opinion. Those who dissent or disagree are viewed as troublemakers, weak, or questioners. Since they are in the minority, they are seen as slow to change and are pushed or coerced into accepting a decision. The few may unwillingly go along with the decision, but this is not unity.

Unity does not constitute "saying the same thing," "agreeing with every issue," or "believing exactly the same doctrine on every point." Unity allows much more than this. Unity provides an open forum for disagreement. Unity begs persuasion and is open to questioning. Unity loves conversation. Unity offers respect to those who agree, disagree, and choose not to decide. Unity seeks consensus but embraces diversity. Unity is direction, not affirmation. Unity involves motion, not sedation. Unity exists under a vision, mission, and calling.

Unity in Ephesians

As a prisoner for the Lord I urge you to live a life worthy of the calling you have received. Be completely humble and gentle; be patient, bearing with one another in love. Make every effort to keep the unity of the Spirit through the shared bond of peace. There is one body, one Spirit (you were called to one hope when you were called), one Lord, one faith, one baptism, one God and father of all who is over all and through all and in all. (Eph. 4:1-6)

This text is considered the "hinge" of the book of Ephesians. The text occurs between the section that emphasizes the Christian's calling to Jesus (Eph. 1:1-3:21) and the section that describes the holiness lived out in the called Christian (4:17-6:24). The vehicle for this unity is gifted leadership (4:11-16). Jesus left gifts of leadership for the church so that Christians can mature through unity.

The Ephesian church was called to unity because they had a common vision and similar qualities/beliefs upon which they could build. They were to bring glory to God and manifest God's love to the world, as well as to the heavenly powers. Since Jesus united all of them, they were to work together to grow and develop spiritually.

Unity Today

Since unity exists under a common vision and seeks to build on common ground, elders can promote unity within the flock, as well as with other congregations, by practicing unity among leaders. Unity should be a core value not only of the church but of the leaders themselves. This means that elders should value a common vision/mission within the leadership. It also means that leaders should seek what they have in common. Elders however, are called to shepherd all the leaders, so they must cultivate vision and encouragement among leaders. Elders are not called to force unity but to develop it. Elders must have unity as a core value so that they can lead others to this same value. Elders can call both leaders and the congregation to unity by promoting vision and encouragement in the church. If their passion is for unity, they will desire harmony.

First, *the elders must promote vision*. Those in leadership who have the gifts of vision from God must be challenged to use them. Dreamers and prophets can make us feel uncomfortable and be intimidating, but vision is their gift and responsibility. Sometimes preachers will call us to move out of our comfort zones to reach the lost. There is nothing worse than a minister who has lost hope, vision, and the ability to dream. The vision of leaders can be a guiding force that unites and drives the church to fulfill the will of God. Elders, as shepherds, can encourage ministers and other leaders who are expected to dream and share vision to feel free to fulfill this divine responsibility. Elders can promote unity by encouraging creativity, trust, faith, and a passion for God's vision.

Elders should not be intimidated by a vision for the future. Ministers are called by God to project the vision for the church and other leaders. When elders and their wives are secure in their faith and spirituality, vision is welcomed and embraced. If they are insecure, vision is resisted and they will fear the future. The Holy Spirit empowers people to dream (Joel 2:28; Acts 2:17). When vision, hope, and the ability to dream are crushed, Satan has a hold on a church. It is important that shepherds guide and encourage those with vision to dream and share their vision with the church.

Second, *elders must encourage those in leadership to build up the body*. Unity may exist under a vision, but unity will always involve hard work. Vision is a gift *from* God. Unity is our gift *to* God. Unity will take hard work, it must be continually maintained. In Eph. 4:3 Paul encourages the church to "be eager to keep the unity of the Spirit through the shared bond of peace." Unity is a desire that takes effort to achieve.

The church is a place for people to grow, develop, and learn. It is a place where people can disagree but also accept their differences. It is a place where we sometimes hold our tongues because we would rather stand together than alone. Unity strives for consensus. Unity loves persuasion rather than coercion.

After a second warning, Paul called on Titus to remove the divisive people (Titus 3:10). The definition of a heretic is one who causes division. Heretics are

people who disrupt unity. They contribute little to the core values of unity and harmony. They are eager to stir up trouble and cause division. They look for differences
rather than similarities. Though in the end they tear down rather than build up.
They do damage in what they teach. Their fruits are in the damage that they do in
churches. The statement, "It is better to run away and save the fight for another day
than to stay and fight," is true. Elders should encourage leaders and members to
build up the body, but they should also be willing to confront those who are not sincere and harmonious in their attitudes. They have authority to protect the flock.

Third, *elders can encourage reconciliation.* Because the church consists of
humans, there will always be strife and tension. Unity and peace are not the
absence of conflict. Reconciliation brings peace to enemies. Reconciliation
brings mutual respect and support. Reconciliation may involve protecting the
weak and confronting the strong. Reconciliation may involve teaching enemies
to talk and be civil with each other. Reconciliation may be a long process. Reconciliation is modeled in Jesus (Eph. 2:11-19; Col. 1:21-23). Reconciliation involves
conflict resolution, validation, and reinstatement of a relationship.

Person A and B begin to have an issue and stop communicating. In order to
address the problem, or be validated, Person A approaches the *Third Party.*

The *Third Party* offers to talk to Person B, who then gives them an "earful" of
information.

Conflict resolution is an intervention between "warring parties." It is difficult to do because those caught in the middle tend to be "triangulated," which

means that a third party is drawn into the two-party relationship and becomes a stabilizing factor in the dysfunction. For example, when two people experience conflict and one of them approaches a third party. The conflict causes A and B to stop communicating in a healthy manner.

The *Third Party* now is the mediator between the two parties. Instead of A and B talking to each other and working through their problems, they rely on the *Third Party* to solve their problems. The *Third Party* works twice as hard to keep peace. They are involved either because of a feeling of guilt, a fear of allowing conflict to happen so that there can be resolution, or because they are flattered into helping. Use of a *Third Party* makes it difficult to help A and B solve their problems.

Conflict resolution means that the Third Party sets boundaries so that A and B can keep talking and working out their issues. It allows A and B to talk to a *third party* for clarity and support, but the Third Party keeps A and B talking.

PERSON A ←——————————————→ **PERSON B**

THIRD PARTY

Validation means offering support to the one who has been wronged, hurt, or discouraged by another's actions. In Exod. 4:31, the people were able to worship because they were validated by God. God claimed to see their suffering, and this support gave them a renewed sense of worship. Today, many in the churches are told to "get over it" or confront another themselves. This is not always possible. Those who oppress and hurt others must be confronted and taught to have empathy for the suffering of others as a result of their actions. Timothy was called to confront and rebuke elders who had sinned if two or three had come to him concerning their sin (1 Tim. 5:19-20). In many cases those in power are unapproachable. People are not able to confront them due to their own fear or power held by the leader. Timothy and other leaders were expected to validate the victims by confronting and rebuking leaders who sinned. This public confrontation brought hope to those who were hurt and also served as a warning for others to avoid sinning in the same way. Victims can be supported by leaders. Victims can also be validated by leaders who call those who hurt them to repentance and confession. Those who hurt others either intentionally or unintentionally, need to empathize with those whom they have hurt and validate them through repentance.

Finally, reconciliation involves *reinstating a relationship*. This is not "kiss and makeup," but it is similar. Elders can call members to work to regain the trust and love that existed previously. Elders can call two parties that are at odds to go beyond peace or a "cease fire" and work toward true unity. This also prepares members to work through future conflicts and problems. It takes time and requires each person to work hard to regain the trust of others.

CONCLUSION

Jesus prayed for unity. Paul called the church to unity. Unity is work, but it is also a calling. Unity exists under the vision that God has given for the kingdom, but it must be maintained. People will always have problems and struggles, but they can actively work together to move forward as a team and do their best to leave no one behind. They can work together to not only fulfill the great commission but to grow and develop together in faith and love.

QUESTIONS

1. Why do you believe unity is important?

2. What are the two qualities of unity?

3. Do you believe we as a movement have been committed to unity? Why or why not?

4. How can elders promote and cultivate unity in the church?

5. What are the three methods of reconciliation?

6. What are some deficiencies that you have noticed about your ministry as it relates to this section?

7. What are some of your strengths?

8. What will be your course of action?

Chapter 11

SHEPHERDING DYSFUNCTIONAL FAMILIES

W hy should we include a chapter in this book on dysfunctional families? I believe that this is a growing problem for churches trying to minister in America. We train missionaries in America and send them to other countries, and they expect to experience dysfunction in other cultures. They have learned to work with families in that culture. Today, we see a larger segment of the American population caught in dysfunction. This dysfunction may be due to genetics, trauma, experiences in dysfunctional families of origin, or psychological problems. When one family member or more become dysfunctional, the whole family system is affected.

What is dysfunction? It is interesting to me that family therapists, counselors, psychologists, and child welfare workers have no problem using this term. They have made a clear distinction both in the literature and workshops between dysfunctional and healthy families. Health and wholeness in a family is not a "pipe dream." It is a real possibility. Unfortunately, I have noticed that many Christian counselors, ministers, and church members hesitate to use the term "dysfunctional." I hear, "we're all dysfunctional" or "we're all sinners" almost as if it is an excuse to continue our destructive behaviors within the family and our churches.

Television shows abound with dysfunction. *The Simpsons, Malcom in the Middle, Tool Time, Everyone Loves Raymond, Yes Dear, King of Queens, According to Jim,* and other shows display behavior that is clearly dysfunctional. Pornography, stupid men, bad communication, abuse, verbal humiliation, and other actions seem to cause us to laugh at these families (I have to admit I am guilty of this also). That is why many watch the shows; we like to laugh at our own dysfunction. Yet, we all know that if these families went to therapy, the show would end. It wouldn't be funny or interesting. Unfortunately we learn, as a society, to accept dysfunction as "normal" and believe that *the family staying together* is what is really important.

Yet, those who work with dysfunctional families understand that there needs to be a clear distinction between healthy and dysfunctional. This is important so that the family can change and grow. Currently, one issue for therapists is "who has the right to determine what is healthy and unhealthy?" Yet, counselors still have an understanding of deeply destructive dysfunction and what helps a family be at peace. The definition of a dysfunctional family can be found in this statement:

> A healthy family is a family that addresses dysfunction and works together to overcome the sinful/destructive/unhealthy behavior. The dysfunctional family avoids addressing the dysfunction.

This definition suggests that families work as a team which involves mutual respect, honor, and shared power. This definition also suggests that families improve. Destructive or sinful behavior changes because the one doing this repents and changes their behavior. Those who are affected by this behavior, when validated, work to forgiveness and hold the one with the sin accountable. Health and wholeness are possible. The family has the right to raise the bar of morality and respect within each member. Faith communities, therefore, help families become healthy by encouraging repentance, transformation, grace, forgiveness, and mutual respect. In our churches today, families and individuals need to be shepherded to heal so that children will grow in a safe environment and so that "God the Father" will be seen as one of compassion, empathy, and love.

Family Systems Theory

The Family Systems Theory (FST) provides a unique way of looking at how families interact with one another. FST suggests that all members of a family (and sometimes those of the extended family) interact with one another in the system. The family unit is an emotional system that acts, reacts, and influences the actions of all others in a system.

An example is the dynamic that exists in families of alcoholics. When the father is an alcoholic he is not the only one with a drinking problem, the whole family takes on his problem. He responds by underfunctioning as a husband, father, and man. The mother overfunctions and adapts to his inadequacies by covering for his behavior, protecting the children from his shame and the shame they may receive from outsiders, and becoming both mother and father in the family. She works harder trying to remove the shame that comes from being married to an alcoholic. The children model either the behavior of the mother or father. One child (usually the oldest) may become the "hero" of the family and try to overfunction like the mother. Another child may become the black sheep of the family and refuse to conform to the "code of silence" that exists and is reinforced within the family. Another child may try to break the family tension by becoming the "clown" or "jester" in this family.

This is an example of how one person's sin affects the whole family. While the alcoholic is to blame, the family members adapt and cope in unhealthy ways. This is clearly seen when the alcoholic becomes sober and repents. The spouse of the alcoholic may operate out of fear, guilt, and distrust, and may have a difficult time releasing the control developed over the years. Others may see spouse as controlling, manipulating, and enabling. This is not true. The spouse has only developed unhealthy patterns in order to adapt and maintain a sense of peace and honor in the family. The battle for power does not empower the alcoholic to stay sober. In fact it sometimes provides an excuse to return to the dysfunctional behavior in order to maintain peace. The "hero" of the family struggles later as an adult with perfectionism. The adult "black sheep" becomes a rebel and many times an alcoholic. He/she also continues to have conflict with the mother and "hero" throughout life. The "clown" struggles to avoid conflict as an adult and uses humor to quench feelings of fear, tension, or anger.

All family members have developed a way to maintain equilibrium in the system. Change is difficult, but possible. All members can change the behaviors that they have developed. This is easy for the alcoholic because they have a clearly defined problem. The rest of the family feels that they do not have a problem and sees no need to change. They do need to realize, however, that their adapted behaviors need to be addressed and that all members need to work together for health and wholeness.

Families operate within a system. If a man is an alcoholic, his whole family adapts. If a woman has a gambling addiction, she affects everyone. If one spouse has an affair, the other spouse is humiliated and the children struggle to take sides. If one spouse becomes addicted to pornography the family responds by living in shame and emotional distance. If a man is abusive or controlling or verbally humiliates his wife, his children are emotionally damaged. If a parent abuses or molests their children, the children are affected for the rest of their lives. If couples divorce, everyone is affected. If a child develops a drinking or drug addiction, the parents are affected, even including their personal relationships. The siblings can also be affected by this one child. One sin affects the way the family responds, adapts, and interacts.

While I have ministers and elders tell me that we're all dysfunctional and all families are dysfunctional, I feel that this is not only untrue, it is unbiblical. There are healthy families, and there are dysfunctional families. There are emotionally healthy individuals, and there are dysfunctional individuals. Healthy people address unhealthy issues and make an attempt to change behaviors that hurt others as well as themselves. Dysfunctional families and individuals ignore unhealthy issues and behaviors and try to adapt or adjust. Those in dysfunction are not on their way to health and wholeness. Either they have chosen to continue in sin, or they have become overpowered by the dysfunction and need help to heal. Healthy people are seen when changes take place in their lives over time.

Shepherding Dysfunctional Families

All adults come from and are affected by a family system. Some come from very healthy families and have developed the skills and tools needed to be spiritually whole. They may continue to use these tools in their family or personal system, or they may revert to a dysfunctional way of life. Others come from dysfunctional families and perpetuate the dysfunction in their family or personal system. Still others come from dysfunctional families and adapt to a new family in a healthy way. Whatever the origin, people need to be healthy. Just as dysfunction is modeled, so healthy relationships are modeled.

Elders *must first model healthy family relationships*. Elders must raise the bar as family men. They and their wives must model healthy family relationships. This does not mean that the children do not sin. Often when an elder's son or daughter has to address a pregnancy (from pre-marital sex), addiction, or crisis of unbelief, the logical step seems to be that the elder must resign. He claims that he has not led his family faithfully, takes the blame, and then resigns either to win the child back or as a sign of failure as a leader. I do not believe God has called leaders to do this. The issue is not how perfect or sinless our families are; the issue is how leaders address sin when it is in their home.

Elders can model healthy family relationships not by the "sinlessness" of their children but by how they address sin and help their children restore their relationship with God. Stepping down from leadership only covers the sin. This sends the message that families who have sin do not have to address it. We never blame the elders when members of the church sin. We expect the elders to step up and help members heal. Elders step up in their family by addressing the sin and guiding their children to repentance, forgiveness, and holiness.

Second elders should *understand that everyone has a history*.[158] When elders visit members and spend time with them they can learn about their family of origin, their struggles, and what they want to change and develop as a person in the image of God. The personal time with other Christians can help elders to see what areas need to be strengthened. Elders' wives who work with women of the church are in a unique position in that they can communicate with their husbands the female perspective on how to help couples struggling with dysfunctional issues. Many times men have trouble expressing their feelings or sins while the wives may be more open to share with other women how their husbands may or may not be nurturing the family as God has called them to do (Eph. 5:25-32). Those coming from dysfunctional families of origin can be encouraged to attend men's or women's ministries, parenting classes, small groups, or other spiritual development groups. Elders and their wives can also guide ministers to address issues in sermons or begin ministries that would help those from dysfunction to heal.

Third, elders should realize that *the congregation consists of people with different and sometimes conflicting stories.*[159] Elders and their wives bring their stories into their ministry. If an elder has grown up in family dysfunction and has not become healthy, he will struggle to lead others out of their dysfunction. He may tell members to "suck it up and accept that all families are dysfunctional" since that is how he survived. He may become angry and attack the person who seems to be the source of the problem. If an elder or his wife had a controlling mother, he or she may come down hard on the wife of an alcoholic. If an elder saw his mother abused, he may resent a woman who stays with her abusive husband. If he resented his father, he may not understand the struggles that men face in trying to accept that God has made them emotional creatures. If he grew up avoiding conflict, his anxiety over conflict will not allow him to confront those who need to be challenged.[160] Elders and their wives bring their stories into the ministry of shepherding others.

Finally, elders have the authority from God to *confront those in the congregation who may destroy group dynamics and cohesiveness.* Members who "underfunction" due to dysfunction and sin will cause others to "overfunction" and adapt with unhealthy patterns of behavior. We are all called to love and good works (Eph. 2:10; Tit. 2:14; 3:8). We are called to stir up each other to love and good works (Heb. 10:23-25). We are called to build each other up (Eph. 4:12-16). Those who tear down others, destroy people, or become idle should be encouraged, guided, or challenged to be a team player. People may be selfish as they heal. Yet, we need to guide them to health so that we as a family can go into the world to preach Jesus (Mark 16:14). Elders should confront those who hurt the momentum of our mission and cause members to lose their focus and purpose in the kingdom.

Conclusion

Dysfunctional families are those who do not work toward healing and wholeness. They try to adapt to dysfunction because it seems to be the best or easiest way to keep or maintain peace. It actually has the opposite effect. Dysfunctional families are in great need of healing and spiritual development. Dysfunctional single men and women, those who are divorced, are desperately in need of relationships with healthy individuals. In the past, the burden has been on the minister to bond with members and he in turn became overworked. Today there is a great need for healthy couples to model, shepherd, and guide these men and women who are hurting and in need of strength. Elders and their wives can be a great tool for Jesus if they have become healthy. Churches that become spiritual families with members acting and reacting can promote peace, love, and harmony as if leaders shepherd them to address dysfunction and grow through it.

Questions

1. What is dysfunction?

2. Do you agree with the statement that everyone is dysfunctional or that all families are dysfunctional? Why or why not?

3. What causes family dysfunction?

4. How can elders and their wives help address family dysfunction?

5. After reading this chapter, what are some of the strengths you sense in yourself?

6. What are some of the deficiencies you need to address?

7. How has your family history affected your shepherding? The way you see others?

8. What will be your course of action?

Chapter 12

Shepherding the Congregation: Who Are the Real Predators?

I once knew a man whom I deeply respected. He traveled the world lecturing on evolution and creation. I bought many of his books, listened to his lectures, and was encouraged that a belief in special creation was not for stupid people. I was converted to Christ while in college and was a Biology and Chemistry major. His work and writings helped me study with many of my friends and finish my degrees in a field heavily influenced by evolution. I was thrilled to meet the man after a lecture and talk with him about this issue. He had a profound impact on my life as a new Christian and will always be a major reason why I stayed faithful and finished my undergraduate degrees in science.

I grew a little uncomfortable over time with his heavy attack on doctrinal issues and another scientist's views of evolution/creation. This man, who he was attacking, was equally as popular and influential in my early life. The man I had looked up to waved the banner of doctrinal purity and a stand for the truth. He was fearless and at times, I thought, ruthless but in my mind a great protector of the flock. I read much of his material, as well as his colleagues, and felt that they were defending the flock from predators.

Then, one day, I read the news that this man had been convicted of molesting young boys. I was shocked. I was surprised. I was hurt. I thought of all the young men who looked up to him, read his books, and trusted that he was not only a defender of our faith, but a promoter of Jesus' life. I thought of his victims and I felt pain for them. The betrayal, trust issues, and pain they must have experienced from the "man of God" must have wounded them deeply. I heard very little about validating these victims but I heard a lot from others about how they were shocked. I wondered if these young victims would be OK and if they would still see a loving God now that they had been abused. Then I thought of the man's persistence in attacking false doctrine and error and wondered—*who were the real predators in this story?*

I was at a reception for ministry in a global context. A priest, who was a professor at a university in England, was talking with me about our ministry and work in abuse. "In America, it seems that the Catholic churches are getting hit by a tremendous number of lawsuits for pedophilia. We are saddened that so many victims have been hurt by the priests," he said. "Do you think it is mostly the Catholic Church in America that has this problem?" he questioned. "No," I said. "From our experience it happens in every church. In fact, the Catholic Church is the easiest group to target," I pointed out. He looked puzzled so I further commented, "The problem is big in every religion and country. It's just that the Catholic Church has a more structured system and more detailed records. Basically, the legal system is able to hit the church with the most money and the easiest to trace pedophile behavior." "Interesting," he said. "So you're telling me it is probably as big a problem in all churches?" "Yes," I said, "unfortunately most abuse goes unreported and most churches are autonomous. As we have seen with this issue church leaders tend to ignore the problem so it is hard to prosecute in many other churches that do not have the hierarchy or records of ministers."

We've all heard the stories. A Christian college leader molests his children, a para-church leader is convicted of molesting boys, ministers and elders have sexual affairs with members of their churches, Christian counselors violate patient-counselor conduct through sex, and Christian leaders struggle with alcoholism, pornography, gambling, and other destructive behaviors. I've had women confess to me affairs with and abuses from ministers, seminary students, and church leaders. You have read the stories in the news or watched the newscasts where churches are taken to court by abused victims.

Even worse, we pray for these churches and that God would protect them. We flippantly dismiss victim's accusations as tools of the devil and, even worse—money hungry lawyers. Church insurance companies worry us with stories about "false allegations" even though abuse is underreported and most false allegations are true.[161] We don't believe women and children who confess that they have been targeted by inappropriate behavior. Sometimes youth ministers worry more about protection from false accusation than making sure our kids are safe. I have counseled ministers, elders, and other church members in how to handle an abuse accusation. *I always encourage disclosure to the authorities and validation or protection of victims.* Rarely do both happen. Have we ever wondered why people have a negative view of churches? Have we ever asked what Jesus thinks about the *abusive body* that carries his name? Elders must address all predatory behaviors. Shepherds have spent many years confronting doctrinal predators but have forgotten about the other predators in the church.

The wonderful thing about living in the 21st century is that there are hundreds of books designed to help pastors more effectively shepherd their flocks. What a wonderful resource for our elders who, according to many, have not been trained to pastor the flock. Why read the books? It seems to me that many elders have forgotten who the enemy really is. We do not recognize who the real predators are today.

I became aware that a member of our congregation had been convicted of pedophilia many years ago. I was also aware that he was unmonitored, was still allowed to have children sit on his lap, and was a marriage mentor. He and his wife had offered to keep the children of some of our members without charge and had done so (they once offered to keep our son)! I had not been made aware that he had molested boys in the past and found out that most of our members were also unaware. I was amazed to find out that we had leaders who knew about the problem but treated the situation as if it was not a threat.

While I did not have any evidence that he had re-offended, I was extremely angry and alarmed (to say the least). Upon pressing this issue, one of the elders, in an elders' meeting, looked at me and said, "You're not the pastor of this church." I was hurt, but I also knew that something had to be done. Eventually that elder, myself, a counselor, and another elder confronted the couple and made sure that they kept their distance from children. In our confrontation, more things were revealed that had occurred in the past. We do not know if anyone was molested over the years, but something has always bothered me about this issue and many others like it. Why didn't the elders see this man as a predator, a threat, or a danger to the church? If not, then who did they see as a wolf? I was also troubled that I was criticized by shepherds for wanting to protect the sheep. I was also troubled that if our members ever found out about this issue we would have had a revolt on our hands.

What saddens me even more is that if this man taught controversial issues such as a woman's role in the church, whether we should take communion every Sunday, or baptism and salvation, he would be watched very closely. If he were to teach that salvation comes without or before baptism, he would be visited quickly by some of the leaders. While this is not a critique on what doctrines we believe, it is a critique on how we have traditionally seen predators/wolves in the church. Are our modern-day wolves only doctrinal predators or also sexual predators? Which one presents the greatest threat to the sheep?

This problem of predators in churches is one I constantly face. As a member of local domestic violence councils, the Oregon attorney general's sexual assault task force, and a trainer of clergy for abuse situations I find that abuse and sexual assault are common problems in churches. In fact, most of the churches do not address these sins. Countless women tell me that they have confessed to a leader that their husbands have been abusive and church leaders counsel them to return to their husband. Children share stories of abuse at the hands of a church leader or teacher. Church leaders tell me that they feel they cannot remove a pedophile from their midst and are silent on his sin. Members tell me that accused abusers continue to teach classes, lead public prayer, or stand before the congregation. Even worse than this, I know elders and preachers who do not take a stand to protect victims. I know many leaders who do not confront the abusers.

Abuse prevention advocates indicate to me that the problem is not just that abuse happens in churches, the problem is that church leaders will not confront abuse and protect victims. They also feel that church leaders confront the victims and try to coerce them to forgive. They do not call for justice but allow further victimization. Imagine how terrible it would be to see shepherds ignore the wolves in their midst and feel that their calling is to tell sheep to run from these wolves. They put a band aid on the victims and shake their heads over the loss and suffering of the sheep while the wolves continue to move to other sheep. At some point the sheep will run from the shepherds. At some point God will intervene and save the sheep.

> Therefore this is what *Yahweh* says, the God of Israel, concerning the shepherds who care for my people: "You have scattered my flock, and have driven them away, and you have not attended to them. Behold, I will attend to you for your evil doings, says *Yahweh*. Then I will gather the remnant of my flock out of all the countries where I have driven them, and I will bring them back to their fold, and they shall be fruitful and multiply. *I will set shepherds over them who will care for them, and they shall fear no more, nor be dismayed, neither shall any be missing*," says *Yahweh*.   Jer. 23:2-4

Wolves, Lions, and Predators

Peter tells us that Satan is a lion who devours (1 Peter 5:8). Paul tells us that the wolves will speak distorted truths that will lead people away (Acts 20:29-30). While I acknowledge that our doctrines are important, I believe that we today (as they were in the first century) are living in a world struggling with sexuality. Our most dangerous doctrines involve sexuality, sexual power, and purity.

- In the Churches of Christ it has been estimated that thirty percent of men acknowledge looking at internet pornography on more than twenty five occasions, eighty four percent claims to have viewed pornography, and fifty seven percent claim to have intentionally viewed internet pornography. Three in four men aged nineteen to twenty nine struggle with internet pornography as a temptation.[162]

- One in four women in the United States has been physically abused at least once by her boyfriend or husband.[163]
- One in six men have admitted to being sexually abused as a child.
- One in five women have admitted to being the victim of dating violence.
- One in six women have been sexually assaulted/raped in the US. Young girls aged 11-14 years old comprise the largest group of victims.
- Three percent of college women report being raped during any school year.[164]
- A sexual assault victim is re-traumatized when people do not believe their story.

How many of our men have/are committing the sins/crimes listed above? It is not hard to see where the dangers lie within our congregations. Our churches are prone to sexual sins, abuses, and child molestation. One does not have to look far to see many lawsuits and legal charges against churches that involve children who have been abused or molested by ministers, priests, leaders, camp counselors, or members. It is a growing problem that demands action.

One of our members, Martha, told me a story about her family years ago. The woman and her husband had three children and lived in a small Midwest town. They attended a church where another man took an interest in her children. This man was an active teacher in the church and led many activities with the youth. Her oldest daughter one day confided that the man had been inappropriate with her by touching her sexually. Martha and her husband were outraged and decided to move back to Oregon. Martha's husband went to the men of the congregation and told them what had happened and why they were leaving. Martha looked at me and then said, "One of the older men of the church looked down and said, 'We're sorry—we thought and hoped he wouldn't do it again.'"

"We're sorry. We thought and hoped *he* wouldn't do it again." How should someone accept this "apology?" No one can imagine the anger this couple must have felt. I was angry hearing about it. Martha shook her head and said, "They never told us goodbye. How can anyone let that happen?" Martha's story remains with me today. It is a story that happens often in churches. Preachers, youth ministers, leaders, college professors, college administrators, speakers, doctors, and many others year after year (day after day) prey on children and victimize innocent people. Jesus condemns this behavior.

> If anyone causes one of these little ones, who believe in me to sin, it would be better for him to have a large millstone hung around their neck and to be drowned in the depth of the lake. (Matt. 19:6)

What is even worse, God holds strong condemnation for those who turn their head to these sins.

> If one shuts their ears to the cry of the poor, they too will cry out and not be answered. (Prov. 21:13)

> If a person sins because they do not speak up when they hear a public charge to testify regarding something they have seen or learned about, they will be held responsible. (Lev. 5:1)

In the story of Jacob's daughter, Dinah, Shechem raped and humiliated her (Gen. 34). Jacob was silent and did nothing to protect or fight for her.[165] All of these stories and scriptures tell us that God is not silent on the abuse and oppression of women and children. God's people are called to confront predators and protect victims.

Shepherds Protecting the Flock

How can shepherds and other leaders protect the congregation? If God has called us to speak out, why aren't we doing it? Elders and other leaders must recognize where the greatest threat may be in the church. The false teachers of the Bible mostly focused on immorality and idolatry. Our focus over the years has been on what we call church doctrine. The biblical text calls us to focus on issues that can destroy the emotional health of God's people. The spiritual community must confront issues such as pornography, abuse, molestation, racism, prostitution, and human trafficking. Acts of human-induced trauma are some of the greatest forms of evil among us today. If we want to see where Satan is at his worst, we must look into trauma and abuse issues. We as a faith community are called to confront Satan at this level. The church of Jesus must also confront the power structures of society that further abuse and oppress other human beings.

Insurance companies representing churches have been leading the way in "child protective" issues. These companies have lost money over lawsuits and therefore have become proactive in addressing child abuse and sexual issues. I am thankful that these companies require churches to comply with child safety standards. Unfortunately, I am saddened that the church has not led the way in this area. We can, however, provide an environment for the congregation that communicates safety and love for all of God's people.

First, elders must communicate a *zero tolerance policy* for abuse, pedophilia, power and control over others, and sexual addictions. Empathy and compassion demand this! While we may want to forgive and love the sinner, we must protect the victims. We must not re-victimize others. We must call all people to live the life of *agape* that Jesus called us to live. Those who abuse and oppress others must be confronted by those in leadership. Those who are victims must be validated, supported, protected, and embraced. While we must forgive, we must first call the sinners to repentance. We must call them to empathy and compassion for all of those whom they hurt. Then, in time, forgiveness can come and healing can take place.

Second, we must illustrate *that Satan and evil are alive in these forms of human-induced trauma.* Many times we fail to talk about Satan and evil. Yet in observing the horrible acts of Hitler, Idi Amim, the Serb Milosovic, and many others, we see evil in its most horrible forms. From the slaughter of the Native Americans to the enslavement of Africans, it is clear that humans can commit the most horrendous acts of ungodliness. From the Crusades to the Spanish Inquisition, violence in the name of God was still an act of evil. These acts stay in our minds, but we forget about the silent suffering of many men, children, and women at the hands of humans who are under the influence of Satan. They are sons of darkness and their actions bring nightmares not only to their victims but also to those of us who listen to victims' stories. When we talk about these sins, we must talk about Satan and evil. It is important that we understand that predators, wolves, and lions bring fear to the sheep—as well as to the shepherds. The battles against this evil must consume our time and demand our attention.

Third, *I do believe that there are "doctrinal predators."* Elders and ministers do have the authority from God to confront these troublemakers. However, these teachers have not done the damage on people's emotional, physical, and spiritual lives that pedophiles, abusers, and dysfunctional families have. While I acknowledge that shepherds must beware of false teachers, I believe that most elders are not prepared to address those who potentially oppress other people and prey on those who are vulnerable.

Fourth, we *must encourage preachers and teachers to address these issues* frequently in classes and from the pulpit. Whether we like to talk about these issues or not, there are biblical texts that discuss rape, incest, molestation, murder, human mistreatment, sexual addictions, and child sacrifice. I believe that a high percentage of any church's members have not only experienced these forms of sin, but they know someone now who is experiencing them. Many of our men have experimented with or become involved in these sins. They have crossed spiritual lines into zones of evil and oppression. When was the last time you heard a sermon or were in a class on internet pornography? Have you ever heard the story of Dina or Tamar preached on Sunday morning? How often have our missionaries taken a public stand on human trafficking? These are modern stories and ancient biblical stories. They were issues in the ancient world, and they are still issues today.

Elders must also *embrace those caught in sin*. In Mark 5:1-20, Jesus healed a demoniac who abused people. The demoniac wanted to go with Jesus, but Jesus said to him, "Go home to your family and tell them how much the Lord has done for you and how he has had mercy on you." Jesus did not allow the demoniac to escape his repentance. The man had to return and repent to his community. He had to face those he had abused and validate them. This would have been a long process, but it was what Jesus expected him to do. Elders can hold predators accountable by calling them to repent and validate those they have hurt. These predators can be required to attend counseling or therapy groups. Under the law they can be required to pay their debt to society and go to jail. They can be held accountable in their attempts to give compensation to the victim or to pay child and spousal (ex-spousal) support. Elders can provide a place for these broken people to take responsibility for their actions so that they can heal.

Those who have sexual addictions also need to heal. Pornography is not just about sexual purity; it is about empathy and compassion. It degrades women, and men must learn that women are to be honored and respected as being in God's image. It doesn't matter that the woman chose to be in the photograph. She may have been coerced, she may need money, and she does not understand what she has done to her "sisters of humanity." In fact, she too is caught in the power struggle between good and evil. Viewing her does not help free her from satanic slavery, it further enslaves her. It also enslaves us as men. Pornography says that we as men do not have respect for women and we cannot control our sexual desires. Empathy and compassion tell us that pornography hurts and enslaves all people.

Christian leaders also must be taught empathy and compassion. Leadership has an ethical code—we do not use power to manipulate the vulnerable. Leaders who have sexual encounters with other people (adults or children) are using our power and influence to coerce someone who trusted us because of our authority. Our role is to empower people, not use them for our own gratification. Ministers and elders are especially open to this because we do counsel and talk with women. It is our role to establish healthy boundaries and encourage our wives to work with us. Those who have fallen need to be held accountable and called to repentance. Those who see the temptation to sin need have group accountability with other leaders to prevent an abuse of power.

Elders and ministers must work with other congregational leaders to protect the sheep. In addition to the stories of pedophiles in the church are the horror stories of repeat offenders who move from church to church. The Catholic Church has been paying a heavy price not only for the suffering of abuse victims, but for moving pedophile priests to other Parishes without informing the members. It is very easy for ministers who are dismissed for sexual misconduct, abuse, or other issues to return to ministry in another church without a reference or background check. It is simple for sexual offenders to change churches without leaders sharing these sins with the new church. I have been amazed at how many ministers or other predators have re-offended in another church simply by requesting to teach children or be exposed to women. Shepherds and other church leaders must work together to protect the flock worldwide. This requires an atmosphere of trust between churches and a desire to understand why a person left a church. Leaders can also offer letters of support for those leaving and attending another church. This allows them to share, with the new leaders, some of the strengths and/or struggles a Christian may have and how the new church may help them.

Finally, *we must work with local agencies to address these issues.* Lori and I both spend time leading community agencies and speaking at conferences on the faith community's responsibility to address abuse and sexual assault. I constantly hear that this is rare in the religious world. We have found that our biggest supporters are unchurched community leaders. We firmly believe that God is using them to address this issue. We believe that God would prefer to use the church, but if the church refuses to address it then God will use those outside the community of faith. Why? Since God hates abuse, oppression, sexual assault, and pornography, it is important that we build bridges with our community and work together to stop evil. Churches can shine their light by blessing their cities and helping community leaders grow closer to God.

Elders and ministers can develop relationships with those counseling members for addictions and abuse. They can work with community advocates to help those struggling with sin or those affected by the sins of others to heal and become spiritually whole. Leaders can also take advantage of community resources and gain a better understanding of how to protect those in the flock.

CONCLUSION

Shepherds are called to confront the predators and protect the sheep. Many church leaders have ignored the physical predators in our communities and churches. While some are more concerned about doctrinal error, much more damage has been done by those who destroy the lives of men, women, and children. These predators abuse power and gain control over others. They sexually abuse innocent people. They have sexual addictions and involve others in them. We do not have to look hard to find these predators, they are many times among us. Yet, they can be confronted with love and held accountable. They can be called to validate their victims and make restitution to those who were robbed of their innocence.

QUESTIONS

1. If you were to give a definition of predators/wolves in the flock, what would it be?

2. How have we understood wolves in the past?

3. How can elders protect the flock from wolves/predators?

4. In what ways is your congregation deficient in confronting *wolves*?

5. In what ways is your congregation strong in confronting wolves?

Chapter 13

SHEPHERDING MINISTERS

A minister's wife made national news when she shot her husband. After the news was televised, my wife was interviewed by a newspaper concerning the stress that wives of ministers face. National magazines have done articles about the enormous stress on ministers and their spouses.

Whether we agree with these articles or not, the fact remains that being in ministry presents significant stress and temptations. Ministers struggle with finances, sexual temptations, depression, isolation, work addictions, and other issues that can damage their spiritual health and emotional stability and that of their families. As a minister, I frequently read articles concerning the sins and struggles of ministers. Many ministers fall to sin through internet pornography, adultery, homosexuality, or alcohol addiction, or they experience burnout. While I agree that ministers are human, I believe that we are called to be examples and to model a life of spiritual maturity. These ministers choose to sin but some sins committed by ministers happen due to the pressure and loneliness that the job brings.

My neighbor had come to church a few times, and his wife, son, and daughters were coming fairly regularly. We were talking about our boys' school classes when out of the blue he said, "So, what do you do all week? I mean, it's not like your sermons are all that long. It probably takes you, what, an hour to prepare them?" Holding back a loud laugh, I mentioned that I taught at a college, counseled, visited people, and taught people about Jesus. "You actually get paid to do that?" he asked. "Sure Rick," I laughed because I was afraid if I told him I had a master's and doctorate in this it would have blown him away. I have thought about that conversation often. It did not make me angry—I knew he had no clue what ministers did. He did not grow up going to church. I wonder how many of you have wanted to ask that question.

Christianity Today did article that indicated that ministers, as a whole, are overworked and underpaid for their profession and education.[166] Yet, the journal's survey indicated that the majority of ministers (eighty percent) feel satisfied in their occupations. We know that this is true for almost all ministers. Ministers work and are available all hours. Ministers are constantly on call. Ministers do many different tasks. Ministers, most of us acknowledge, are underpaid for the services they provide. Yet, some label ministers "money hungry" because they want to provide for their families.

Some ministers live in old or poorly maintained parsonages. Ministers get called in the middle of meals, on days off, at nights, and during family time. Ministers get few vacations. Ministers apply for positions and wait, sometimes for weeks, to hear that they are being "considered for the position." Ministers are blamed for declining attendance or weak sermons. Ministers are told, "You have it good since you really only work one day a week."

Ministers are sometimes portrayed as arrogant when they advance their education and ignorant when they choose not to do so. Ministers with doctorates "don't know the word" and "speak over our heads." Ministers are teased when they buy a new car ("Hey, we must be paying you too much . . .") or their children have new clothes. Ministers are "whiners" if they ask for a raise. Ministers have to find their own insurance. Retirement—what's that?

Am I exaggerating? Actually, I am speaking from personal experience. I am not only sharing what has been said of me, I am sharing what I have heard in church business meetings. I am sharing what elders have said to me about other ministers. I acknowledge that there are many churches taking care of their ministers. But I also acknowledge that there is a shortage of ministers. Men are leaving the pulpit, and fewer young men are going to school to fill these empty pulpits. We have a problem.

Many ministers and their wives suffer because they are not shepherded by their elders. Every year countless ministers fall by choosing internet pornography, adultery, alcoholism, and other sins over their commitment to Jesus, their family, and the church in which they serve. Other, with their families, suffer burnout and struggle to set healthy boundaries.[167] Sometimes the wives stand in the shadows of the "preacher" and become lost in the crowd. Sometimes their children fulfill the role and stereotype of the preacher's kids (PKs) and resent the church, the faith, and God. The church leaders and families who need shepherding the most wither on the vine. They long to be shepherded but have to fulfill the stereotypical role of *Pastor*. Many ministers are converts to Christianity and cannot depend on their biological fathers to guide them spiritually. They have what is called "the father wound." These men struggle for approval from other men and can become addicted to hard work and performance. If they work with men who withhold attention and affection they focus on working harder to receive this attention. My father never heard a sermon that I preached. I believed he loved me but didn't care about my ministry. This has affected my outlook on myself and has made me sensitive to criticism and a people-pleaser or "rescuer" in my work. It has also given me a desire to be validated by men in what I have chosen to do for God. I acknowledge that I need shepherding from mature men. I have had other young ministers share similar feelings. We do expect maturity from older men because we know how immature older men have hurt us and caused us to become disillusioned by their sin and dysfunction. It seems that some elders have repeated the tragedy of "absent or distant fathers" when it comes to shepherding ministers and their wives.

A friend of mine who is a Lutheran minister and works with abusive men was talking with me about our system of church leadership. When I expressed that our elders try to set the direction of the congregation, he indicated that this will never work. "You cannot give ministry decisions to lay people who have not learned a good theological paradigm as you have." Later we began to talk about how ministers struggle with loneliness and sin. His wife echoed that she had been neglected in the past as a "Pastor's wife." He also expressed his suffering. "Who pastors the Pastor?" he asked. "That is why we have elders," I said. "They shepherd the minister and wife as couples and develop a relational dynamic with men and women in the church." Part of what my friend said was true. We should encourage trained ministers to guide the vision and mission for the church. They have been given that authority by Jesus (Eph. 4:11-16). Many also have the theological training. We either value academics or we do not.

How often have we talked with those married to ministers? How often have we talked with their children? Are we aware of the pressures that these families face? We tell stories and jokes about PKs (preacher's kids), but how much of the "wild PK behavior" is due to family dynamics? What is it like to live in a fishbowl? Even more, what is it like to live under the financial strain which many ministers' families endure? I understand that all families face difficulties, but we know that minister's families have multiple stress factors in their homes and their congregations. We know that ministers' wives who suspect their husbands of sin feel alone and vulnerable to sin, judgment, and isolation. I have had countless adult children of ministers tell me that they vowed never to enter ministry because they watched their father labor for pennies. They felt that their father was committed first to God, the church, the community, and then to their family. Instead of being advocates for ministers when these children become adults and move to a church, they expect the ministers to be treated the same way as their father was treated.

A wonderful widow of a preacher I greatly admired told me something very personal. I was visiting her with my little boys, and she began to confess that she and her children had felt neglected when her husband was in ministry. She said that in the family it was understood that God was first, the church second, and the family third. She did not blame just her husband, but the unwritten codes of conduct that existed for ministers many years ago. She encouraged me to take my boys visiting but also to remember that Lori and my sons needed me. She reminded me that their view of God, church, and ministry would be dependent upon my investment in *their lives* rather than the church. What a challenge!

I know it may seem that I am complaining. I do not intend to do that. I know it may seem that I am airing out dirty laundry. Maybe I do intend to do that. I do want to communicate something important in this chapter. If elders are called to shepherd the flock and protect the weak, then who is most in need of this protection? If we want ministers to be on the front lines, how concerned are we about their spiritual, emotional, and physical well being? If we want ministry families to stay strong, how concerned are we about their health and wholeness? Of all the people in the congregation, I believe that ministers (especially missionaries) and their families should be a high priority for elders. How often have we spent high amounts of our energy with families that will continue to struggle with sin and neglect others who truly need it?

All people need shepherding. All people struggle with temptation. Some people need shepherding because they are aggressively fighting Satan and evil. Those people will continue to make great strides for the kingdom because they are shepherded. Rather than assuming that they will be fine because they are aggressive, we should assume that they need reinforcement and guidance because they are at great risk. They are at risk not because they are tempted more; they are at risk because they are "targets" in the battle between good and evil. They are at risk because they are supposed to be on the front lines and therefore are in the heat of battle.

A Plea from a Preacher!

This chapter is different than the others. This is a heartfelt plea. In all the books I have read concerning ministry, elders, or church growth, I have read little about shepherding ministers. I am upset about the declining number of ministers in the pulpit. I am upset at the ministers who do not take a "day off" during the week for themselves and their families. I am alarmed by the graduates who choose the academy over the pulpit ("Are you crazy? The politics of ministry are not for me!"). I am concerned about the preachers who choose sin over the task of modeling Jesus. I am saddened by the increase in the number of ministers' wives struggling with depression and loneliness. I grieve over the neglect that they have to face while standing in their husband's shadow. I see countless more take jobs and become less and less involved in their husband's ministry (they hired him not me).

It is not all doom and gloom, but we need to be alarmed at the gloom. The gloom is bad, and it will kill our churches. The gloom damages ministers' kids and those close to ministry families. This is the reason for this chapter. I want us to realize the seriousness of this issue.

Elders and their wives ought to seriously consider spending time mentoring and shepherding their ministers. The struggle for power is not due to individual strengths as much as it is to individual weaknesses. Those who vie for power do so because they feel deficient in power. The hunger for power comes from insecurity, not confidence. Elders and ministers can work as a team with other leaders when the shepherds take the time to guide those in ministry.

First, *ministers are called to vision and proclamation*. Elders need to cultivate this in ministers. Your preachers need to be calling you out of your comfort zone and modeling the incarnation in the community. Your preachers need to be pushing you to be the best you can be. They are not the enemy, and you are not in charge. They are fulfilling a task that God has sent them to do.

Second, *ministers need to be pushed* to grow intellectually and spiritually and also at home. Just as they challenge you, you can challenge them. They need to remember their family. They need vacation time. They need to be left alone. They need to get away with their wives. They need to go with their sons and daughters to Disneyland and every other place you have gone. They need to sleep in. They also need to go to workshops, seminars, and classes. They need to grow like every other man in the church.

Candace R. Benyei suggests that ministers also struggle with personal dysfunction.

> In a 1988 study with high functioning clergy 91 percent reported chronic physical dysfunction and problems with weight in their own or their spouse's family of origin, 83 percent reported chronic emotional disorder and suicide attempts, 75 percent reported diminished sexual interest and acting-out children, 66 percent reported substance abuse,

58 percent reported affairs/illegitimate children and problems with the law, 50 percent reported chronic or episodic physical violence, 25 percent reported incest, and 8 percent reported compulsive gambling.[168]

While these studies were done with various denominations, experience tells us our churches are similar to what Benyei is reporting. Ministry attracts a very feeling and highly driven individual. It is extremely easy for ministers to become rescuers and heroes in both their minds and the eyes of the church. Oswald and Kroeger suggest that clergy have tremendous temptations to abuse members sexually because:[169]

➢ They are expected to be intimately involved in the life of parishioners
➢ They are expected to be open, vulnerable, and share this—this can encourage entanglement
➢ Loneliness an isolation increase the temptation
➢ 70% of the studied clergy are Feeling types, on the Myers/Briggs personality profile (male and female) which makes them more likely to be enmeshed in people's lives
➢ They can become lost in caring, irrational, and not concerned about long term consequences
➢ As Feelers they can be attractive to parishioners who are needing love and support

Benyei also indicates that the minister's family of origin influences the way the minister relates to his family as well as the church. Ministry does attract those who come from dysfunction and provides a chance for us to help others heal. However, it is important that the "healer" is placed on a spiritual "HMO" and guided by shepherds who will help him and his family become what God has called them to be. It also is important for elders to realize that highly functioning clergy, while doing great work for the church, are also at risk for damaging behaviors.

If the research on the crisis of male leadership is any indication of our society, we can assume that many ministers struggle with what it means to be a man. My father was an atheist, and he struggled to be a good father. He did the best he could, but when he died I realized it wasn't good enough. He did the best he could from where he came, but there is no excuse for the bad he did. Becoming healthy means that we acknowledge sin, condemn it, and repent of it. I have had to acknowledge my need for male spiritual leadership as I grow. Older men have failed to lead and have disappointed me, as my dad did. Some older ministers and other leaders have failed to be what I need in a male example. Other men have been great fathers to me. They have taught me to be what I need to be and what God desires me to be. I have decided to never fail younger men, ministers, interns, or even my sons the way that some of our leaders have failed us. One way to accomplish this is to seek spiritually mature men who will help me grow.

> Let those of us who are mature think this way; and if in anything you think differently, God will also reveal that to you. Only let us hold true to what we have attained. Brothers and sisters, join in imitating me, and mark those who live this way so that you have an example from us. Phil. 3:15-17

Paul calls the church to seek relationships with those who model a mature spiritual life. This especially applies to ministers who need leaders to mentor them. Ministers still need guidance from other spiritually healthy men.

Third, *ministers' wives and families need to be mentored*. Most of them cannot go to family for babysitting, for advice, or to talk about their husband (I believe it is healthy for all of us to have an outlet). Ministers' wives are some of the loneliest women in the church. They stand in the shadows of their husband. Many have given up careers to stay at home with the children or to support their husband in ministry. Many are "expected" to stay home and do so on a fixed income. Sometimes people see nothing wrong with complaining to them about the minister. They listen to people continually talk about "his ministry" or how "he" is a great leader. These women are neglected. Lori tells me that even though I try to call it "our ministry," people still talk about what "Ron" does or "Ron's" church.

These women are guarded in their relationships. They try to protect their families and husbands. They try to be careful because they hold many secrets. They many times bite their tongue when a single woman brushes past them to talk to their husband, compliment him, or ask for his time. They listen to us when we vent, but they act as if everything is fine. They are wise, perceptive, and strong but very vulnerable. They need support and love from elders and their wives.

The children also need help. Sometimes they see their father as the only leader in the church. No matter how much I tell my sons about elders, they only see what goes on in the home. We have a few elders and their wives who have developed relationships with my boys. My sons can talk with them if they feel at odds with me or Lori. My boys have spent time in their homes when Lori and I go out on a date. These couples watch my boys' activities and take an interest in them. These couples have been a great blessing to my family. When elders and their wives develop relationships with these children, they provide a broader perspective on church leadership and help the children develop adult relationships aside from their parents.

Finally, *ministers will stay a long time in churches where they feel supported, encouraged, and effective.* I have heard and read the statistics concerning longevity of the minister and health/growth of a church. I understand that ministers who stay long term in a church have an effect on the growth and stability of a congregation. I also know that ministers who stay a long time in congregations where they are not supported will become stale and ineffective. The key to longevity is not the minister "sticking it out." The key is elders who support, encourage, and challenge him to grow spiritually. The key is providing a support network for his family. The key is helping his wife connect with women leaders and other women in the body. It will always be hard for a minister to leave a church with leaders who provide strong emotional and spiritual support.

In a conversation with a church growth specialist, I voiced my concern that we often encourage ministers to stay in unhealthy situations too long because of the belief that longevity is the key to turning the church around. He was silent at first and then said, "Well, ministers just need to quit griping about their salaries and stay longer in churches."

I was bothered by this comment because it assumes that the problem rests solely on the ministers. If leaders and other church members feel that ministers gripe too much about salaries, are greedy, and will leave when the next best offer comes along, why do we hire them? If we resent them and don't trust them, we will never grow. We will always be on different pages theologically. We will never be compatible until we listen to each other and understand why we hurt.

When we work together, we will see growth. When elders and their wives embrace ministers as partners, rather than foes, we will see healthy churches. When ministers feel connected and supported, they have a greater chance of staying long term in the congregation. When we work as a team, we become united against Satan.

Accountability and Unity

I was refereeing at the district wrestling tournament and serving as an assistant referee during a match. The winner went to the state tournament, the loser placed fourth and his season was over. It was a tense match and the coach was yelling that the referee had made a bad call. The coach and I got along well and I respected him. He was a good, fair, and knowledgeable coach. As assistant referee, I could not address him.

"Coach, you'll need to address the referee, you know you can't talk to the assistant . . ." I said. "Yah, yah, I know—he's a rookie and he made a bad call. You saw it, you can tell him," he yelled. He was right, I could talk but the assistant can only confer when asked. The rules are clear. The referee was a rookie, but I didn't see the call. I suspected, by the way the match was flowing that he might have missed a call.

The coach's wrestler won his match and went to state. But the coach was a fair man and approached me after the match. "Hey, I'm not mad at you and I know you guys stick up and support each other, but you can't make a call like that. These kids don't deserve to miss out on state because a ref makes a lousy call." He was right, but I didn't see it and he didn't believe me. No matter how many times I said, "I honestly didn't see it," he saw me as loyal to referees, not the kids. I guess it many times looks like we support each other, even if the call is bad. I reminded the other official later that he needed to be on his toes and accountable for any calls he made.

The same is true in church leadership. First, people are important. While it is important that we serve God we understand that if the people are hurt (inside or outside the church) then we are not doing our job. Too often leaders get caught fighting or arguing with each other or even neglecting the people. In the end, the people are hurt. We are called to serve God and people. We are to empower people to wrestle with God and decide the outcome. Faith will be between them and God, not us. Therefore we provide a place of safety and security for them to grow and develop their faith.

Second, leadership has a standard to uphold. Too often newer elders feel intimidated as they become shepherds. In some cases they are made to feel that way. Yet, biblically they have earned the right to lead and should raise the bar for other leaders. In some cases elders allow those who have been shepherding to continue in unhealthy patterns of ministry. All elders should be seen as mature Christians who are there to lead and guide the church to grow and develop. We support each other, but we uphold the standard that God has set before us. In 1 Timothy 5, the evangelist is told to rebuke elders in sin. How often does this happen? All leaders should have permission to encourage each other but also to rebuke each other "in the presence of others so that the rest may stand in fear/respect." We guide each other to be better and most of the time we do that through encouragement. We help identify errors but also focus on the strengths and what we are doing well. Just as the coach pointed out that my silence could hurt the kids, so our silence on the sins of leadership, can also hurt the people we serve.

Elders and their wives should not hold back the vision of the church or the giftedness of other leaders. Their responsibility is to encourage people to reach their giftedness and fulfill their mission for Christ. Their position is not one of power or control. They are to empower and encourage others to be what God has called them to be. Older leaders should empower newer leaders to grow and believe in the vision of Christ. They are not leaders who become entrenched in tradition—they are leaders who raise the bar for, mentor, and guide other leaders to fulfill the mission of Christ.

The standard we uphold brings glory to God. The standard we uphold brings respect to the positions of elder, minister, and other leadership positions. The standard we uphold also makes it possible for the members to grow, develop, and conquer sin in their lives.

Conclusion

Elders and ministers over the years seem to have had a love/hate relationship. There seems to be competition over who is in charge. While this is not the case for all minister/elder relationships it does seem to be common. One way to avoid this is for elders to shepherd their minister and his family. Elders and their wives can provide valuable emotional, spiritual, and physical support for ministry families, who face tremendous stress. Shepherding these couples not only helps them to grow, it provides a long term relationship which in turn blesses the church. It also helps to bless families in ministry so that they can stand together with the elders to fight Satan and withstand many of the darts the enemy shoots our way.

Questions

1. In your opinion, have I described accurately the stereotypes that people have concerning preachers and their families? Explain.

2. Have I accurately described the stress and strain that ministers' wives face? Explain.

3. Explain how you have shepherded your minister(s) and his family?

4. What areas do you feel you or the leadership in the church need to address in ministering to ministers and their families?

5. Describe a plan that you have to shepherd your minister and his family.

Chapter 14

THE FUTURE OF SHEPHERDING

One of the values of an elder development ministry is that it looks to the future. We identify, train, and develop elders because we want to prepare leaders for the future and we want to be prepared for the future. The task of developing elders can never be something that only "passes on traditions." While the apostle Paul gave instructions, traditions, and an example of how Christians were to live (1 Cor. 11:1; 2 Thess. 3), he was more concerned with preparing Christians to live in their cultures. Paul was a former rabbi who lived under human laws, decrees, and traditions. He was not interested in creating another legalistic system similar to the one in first century Judaism. Paul felt that leaders equipped the church to live in the world and be examples of Christ's love (Eph. 4:12-16).

The task for leadership includes not only mentoring other leaders, but preparing others to lead in succeeding generations. Our job is to train others to take the gospel of Jesus to each generation, culture, and part of the world. This means that we do more than train them to uphold the way we have led. We train them to use the same tool that we use. Since we believe that the Bible is the inspired word of God, (2 Tim. 3:16) we apply it to our contexts. Since we believe that the Bible is authoritative for all people and generations, we train our leaders to apply it to their contexts.

ELDERS OF THE FUTURE

I am convinced that the battles my children and the next few generations will fight will be different than mine. My past battles have been fought over which church is closest to the truth, whether or not baptism is essential for salvation, and the issue of divorce and marriage. Since moving to Oregon, my discussions have been with atheists, Satanists, new age gurus, liberal theologians, and gay/lesbian/transgender believers. These discussions center on the authority of God, Jesus, and the Bible. My battles have been fought over whether abused women should be protected or sent back to their abusive husbands. My battles involve helping men to be compassionate and empathetic in their lives and relationships with others. They have been fought over protecting children and confronting evil in the form of human rights violations. Even more than that, I have fought to convince God's people that they should break out of their comfort zones and reach the lost. The battles I have fought and the issues I have had to face in Oregon are much different than those of the rural areas in Missouri.

In reading books about Postmodernism and the new age, I suspect that the battles we will fight twenty years from now (Lord willing) will be much different. Still the weapons will be different, the location will be different, and the questions will be different. Two things will remain the same. First, the enemy will always be Satan. Second, the word of God will always be our sword against evil (Heb. 4:12; 1 Peter 1:23). The future is not dependent on how well we know the enemy but on how well we use our sword (2 Tim. 3:17). The future is also dependant on how we engage, love, and empower others in the world to seek Jesus.

Yet the books about Postmodernism tell us that we have entered a world/culture that has rejected our old way of thinking. While Modernism praised science, rationality, and reason, deep down we all knew that *agape* was not logical, science was limited, and the lament of Psalms, Lamentation, and Job could never be subjected to a rational thought process. God was always present in the mystery and ambiguity of life. Postmodernism is ready to embrace what we have neglected.

Postmoderns love narrative. This comes from a generation without a spiritual history. Most young people today are not raised going to church, unless an evangelistic friend invited them, and they have little knowledge of the Bible, the church, and spirituality. This generation needs not only to hear the story, but it needs to see it in the lives of Christians. This generation without a story rejects authority because authority requires tradition and familiarity with leaders. Leaders have the great opportunity to earn the respect of this generation and live the story of Jesus for everyone to see. We are a generation with precepts, principles, and examples (you thought I was going to add necessary inference, didn't you?). They are a generation that wants something real that they can experience.

Postmoderns seek spiritual things. They want to experience worship and the presence of God. While they can believe that the word is God's divine revelation, they want to see this revelation in Jesus and God's people. Incarnation is the best way to reach postmoderns because they want to experience God's nature. Leadership needs to be real and willing to touch people's lives.

Postmoderns value community. I am convinced that this is one of the strengths of this culture, and it is more biblical than the model we have stressed. As modernists, we have pushed the Western envelope. The Eastern Church was very oriented toward community and groups. Western culture and the church at Rome eventually gained power in the church and has dominated our theology for many centuries. Western culture is individualistic, rational and reason oriented, and power focused. This led to scriptural interpretation becoming a matter of private judgment and a logical pattern or process. Leadership, like the Roman Empire, became about power and control rather than empowerment. My friends who specialize in church history indicate that this shift brought the focus on the cross and shame in the Christian movement. While the Eastern Church focused on community, mystery, and the resurrection, the Western church continued to dominate the theology of Christianity.

Postmoderns or emerging Christians embrace social justice.[170] I have listened to people criticize this generation as a generation without morals. I have heard that this group believes that truth is relative. I disagree. This generation will stand and condemn us (including me) for turning our head to racism, violence, materialism, misogyny (disrespect for women), economic oppression, sexual and domestic abuse, human sweatshops, and human trafficking in both America and abroad. Those were *our relative truths* and we suffer for them. Historically the *Greatest Generation* and we *Baby Boomers* turned our heads to these issues in our churches. I am excited that our young people have the courage to dream about peace, equality, and empowerment. Starbucks has a better plan for equality and social justice than most of our churches. In fact, I believe that God is using many relief agencies because churches have failed to fulfill the ministry of Jesus in our communities. While we may claim to have God, we need to ask if God has us.

I am also glad that this generation wants to return to Luke/Acts in the study of Jesus.[171] I have heard the term "social gospel" used as a negative to any church trying to become involved in their community. We are told that our responsibility is to "preach the gospel and save souls, not the social gospel." Yet anyone who reads about the Jesus of Luke and the church of Acts has to acknowledge that Jesus had a social gospel. Anyone who reads the prophets has to acknowledge that God has a social gospel. We also know that the Greeks made the distinction/separation between body and soul but the Jews saw soul and life as the same thing. It is a package deal. To care for someone's life is to care for their soul. Jesus heals and says that they are "saved."

This generation has seen our hypocrisy and knows that we label "social gospel" as anything that calls us to be involved with people and affect our community. It is also a term used by non-growing churches about churches that are growing. It is an excuse for lack of growth. It is a label that communicates cowardice. I am abhorred when I hear this excuse, but acknowledge that the church of the future will empower our communities to bring glory to God. Therefore, leaders of these churches must also bring awareness to the suffering of people in our communities and how we as a church might bring healing and transformation to their lives and our cities.

Postmodernism can bring a fresh reevaluation and reexamination of our faith to the forefront. While postmodernism has its faults, it can bring us back to the Bible to pull out texts and spiritual meaning for a lost world. Postmodernism causes us to reevaluate our preconceived ideas when approaching the text and forces us to look at the text from a different perspective. Those who wish to lead and minister to this generation must be prepared to reengage the biblical text and struggle to interpret it and apply it to our world today.

Preparing Elders for the Future

Preparing elders for the future begins with the current leadership. First, *elders must practice self-care and spiritual health.* As mentioned earlier, elders who are dysfunctional cannot model healthy spirituality for others who are dysfunctional. Elders who are not mature or spiritually strong cannot lead others to spiritual maturity. Elders who are weak or experiencing burn-out will only make matters worse if they try to help others. Elders must be *praying and reading the Bible daily* in order to draw closer to God. They need this time with God and in the word.

Elders *must take times of rest and Sabbath* with their wives, children, and grandchildren. They cannot neglect them. The work of shepherding can be overwhelming. In Luke 4:42-44, Jesus intentionally said no to the good work of healing because he knew his purpose. Saying no to church business and yes to family time, dates with spouses, and spending a quiet evening at home are essential. These are times of rest that God provides leaders in order to recover.

Elders *must recognize when they are overwhelmed and share the burden.* Being an elder does not mean that one takes all of the problems and joys of the congregation on one's shoulders. Elders must work together with their spouses and with other leaders. Elders should delegate much of the work and encourage others to join with them in ministering to the church. When one feels tired, empty, dry, or apathetic, it's a good sign that he needs a break.

Second, elders can prepare for the future by *recognizing their culture.* Elders need to know about current issues, media, and temptations that Christians face. When visiting, elders can talk with young men and women about what they are struggling with. They can listen to their opinions about their world and how the church should respond. They must engage people and the world. They must value human relationship and regularly interact with people. Since media is one of the most common indicators of our culture, elders can wisely choose movies, television shows, and music as a point of intersection. Instead of shutting out our world, elders can learn from our world what members think and feel about life and God.

Third, elders can *seek out potential leaders*. My opinion is that the best potential leaders are good husbands and good fathers. These are the men with the most potential because these behaviors are hard to develop. These are the ones who we see displaying compassion and empathy. They will embrace the command to love others and share their faith with outsiders. You can spend a solid year in the Bible and have a good understanding of the Christian life and faith, but it takes years to develop good parenting and spousal skills. Too often we look for those who know the Bible, but we neglect the moral qualities and family values. The future of the church is dependent on what type of men we have as leaders.

Finally, elders can *empower newer leaders to dig into the word of God, engage our culture, and provide fresh thinking*. If the future of the church depends on our ability to go to other cultures and generations, then we need to prepare the leaders of the future to go with God. Once a person becomes a leader, they should be spiritually mature. Yet, spiritually mature people realize that they are dependent upon the word of God. They understand that their strength comes from God's Holy Spirit, and the Bible. Those who continue to study the Bible learn more and more about how to apply it to daily life. The greatest gift a leader can pass on to another is a desire for the Word and a new way of thinking.

Younger leaders can be encouraged to raise the bar of expectations for our leaders. Instead of passing on policies, statements of faith, or articles of incorporation (although sometimes these have to be done), older elders can empower newer elders to search the biblical text and ask questions. An open environment that welcomes discussions, questions, and challenges will provide all leaders the opportunity to search for answers in a changing world. In this environment, change is welcome.

CONCLUSION

This next generation is comfortable with change. In fact, this next generation has come to expect change. Leadership will always be called to engage this postmodern culture and find a way to present the gospel of Jesus. Elders can look to the future by empowering younger leaders to find answers to current issues through the Word of God. This means that leaders must be comfortable in their relationship with God and must be people of the Word. Leaders can practice incarnational leadership by engaging this culture and seeking ways to empower others to take the gospel of Jesus into a changing world. Elders can only empower others, and by faith, pray that the next generation will carry on the tradition of incarnational leadership. This means that the church of the future may look different than it does today, but it also means that the church of tomorrow will be empowered to unashamedly engage the biblical text and culture in their reflection of Jesus.

QUESTIONS

1.What are the differences between Modernism and Postmodernism?

2.How can elders prepare leaders for the future?

3.In what ways have you been prepared for the future?

4.In what ways have you not been prepared for the future?

5.What issues do you feel will need to be addressed by leaders in the next twenty to thirty years?

Chapter 15

SUGGESTED ELDER DEVELOPMENT PROGRAM

In the first section I hope that I made a strong case for developing elders in the church. In section two I tried to encourage a newer direction for elder development, namely a focus on moral and family values. In this third section I included a few of the many issues that elders and their wives need to address. While not exhaustive, it is an attempt to get others talking about training other leaders.

I have led an elder development ministry during my eight years as preaching minister for the Metro Church of Christ in Gresham, Oregon. During this time I have seen eight men identified, developed, and appointed to this task. I have seen our elders take the lead in many ministries and aggressively pursue people in their struggles here in Oregon. I have observed the elders' wives ministering to our women and developing various women's ministries with singles, parents, divorcees, retirees, and young married women. I can testify that an ongoing elder development ministry constantly provides a church with couples who are prepared for the task of shepherding. The new elders begin their task at full speed and try to raise the bar when it comes to performing the task. I have enjoyed watching them serve the flock and bring joy to many people. In fact, I would say they have gained a good reputation in both the church and community.

What began as a doctoral project has now become an ongoing training program. One quarter every year (Wednesday nights) we offered various trainings to elders and their wives and those seeking the position. It was always well attended and a great opportunity for our elders to identify younger couples who are considering this ministry. The trainings varied from year to year, but they were designed to help prepare the elders and their wives for ministry to their current generation.

As Lori and I began a new church plant on the other side of Portland with the Agape Church of Christ, we know that elder development will continue to be one of our passions. It will be exciting seeing new faces and identifying new couples to train for the future. I think that much of our ministry will be the same, but it will also be ministry at a different level. Every church is different, and every elder development ministry is unique. I would like to leave an outline of what we covered in our trainings that you might find helpful in your ministry. Feel free to adapt it to your setting or rearrange it however you would like. The intent is to present these couples with fresh material that will give them the skills to help those in the church who struggle with the many issues that we face today.

First year/cycle: What Is Elder Development?

In this cycle, we discuss much of what I have addressed in chapters 1-7. We try to give the men and their wives a different perspective on elders and identify the need for elders and the moral/family values that must exist. This should consume your first year/cycle because it is a newer way of preparing elders. You will also identify some of the strengths and weaknesses in those attending. Time should be given to the men and women to help them overcome their deficiencies and enhance their strengths. This is an important time to develop a theology of shepherding for your congregation.

The books listed below are solid books for any elder or potential elder. They are standards for our movement and do an excellent job of identifying the characteristics of elders as well as the issues that elders will face. A heavy study of the Pastorals (1 Tim., 2 Tim., and Titus) will also enhance the training. 1 Peter 5 and Eph. 4:11-16 can be addressed, but they are studied deeply in other cycles.

Suggested reading:

Lynn Anderson, *They Smell Like Sheep*
Ian Fair, *Leadership in the Kingdom*
Alexander Strauch, *Biblical Eldership: An Urgent Call to Restore Biblical Church Leadership*

Second year/cycle: Faith Development

This cycle is an opportunity to teach the class how to develop their faith as well as the faith of the members. Chapters 7, 9, and 10 of this book address faith development and unity in the church. This year/cycle is a perfect time to talk with leaders about getting involved within the lives of members and helping them develop spiritually. Sell's book does an excellent job of identifying major faith issues for all people at various stages of life. Gunz's manual is from Great Commission Resources and has been an effective and practical manual for our elders.

Ephesians is a good text to study during this period. The class can give a strong emphasis to this book, especially chapter 4:1-16. 1 Corinthians can also be a supplement to this study.

Suggested reading:

Charles Sell, *Transitions Through Adult Life*
Curt Gunz, *Shepherding: Ten Ways to Be a More Effective Elder*

Third year/cycle: The Church as Family

This year/cycle is also a good time to focus on working with the members and their family of origin issues. Richardson's book is an excellent resource on how the Pastor (he uses the traditional definition) can work with the various personality and emotional dynamics within a church. Balswick and Balswick provide a great introduction to helping families, which I think should be a resource for all Christians, especially leaders. Cruse's book is a great illustration of what it means to help families caught in alcoholism. It is easy to understand and easy to apply to all dysfunctional families.

Ezekiel 34 and Jeremiah 23 are good beginning texts to introduce the class to the need to be personally involved in the lives of the sheep. A deep study of 1 Timothy and Titus (which may be a review for some) is also applicable to this cycle.

Suggested reading:

Ron Richardson, *Creating a Healthier Church*
Jack O. Balswick and Judith K. Balswick, *The Family: A Christian Perspective on the Contemporary Home*
Sharon Wegscheider Cruse, *Another Chance: Hope and Health for the Alcoholic Family*

Fourth year/cycle: Elders and Our Modern Church

The book by Fleer and Siburt is a recent resource that has come from the Elder Link sessions. Abilene Christian University has been emphasizing elder trainings for a few years and has done an excellent job exposing elders to current theological and church issues. Dodd, while not a member of the Restoration Movement, places an emphasis on the spiritual power of leaders. His book is an attempt to call leaders away from a modern "business model" of leadership to a spiritual and theological model.

In this cycle, a deep study of 1 Corinthians will draw the participants into discussions of issues that modern elders face. It will be a great time for newer ideas and applications to be discussed in class.

Suggested reading:

David Fleer and Charles Siburt, *Like a Shepherd Lead Us*
Brian J. Dodd, *Empowered Church Leadership*

Fifth year/cycle: Power and Empowerment

Using the basic model of power and control for abusive families, we can identify potential problems when leadership does not empower the congregation. All the books listed below deal with male power in our society. This cycle provides an opportunity to introduce leaders to the difference between controlling others and being men of peace. This will also be an opportunity to discuss men's and women's ministries in the congregation and how to help families in high dysfunction. In my experience as a domestic violence educator, verbal and physical abuse and control are extremely common in Christian families.

Katz, Miles, and Livingston provide the best material concerning helping men be peaceful. I have listed my book only because it is the only resource published within the Restoration Movement perspective. 1 Peter is a good book to study concerning men, and Ezekiel 34 explains the abuse of power that the shepherds committed in the church. This cycle will help the elders develop specialized ministries to empower victims in our churches and communities, and to help men heal from their past victimizations or their sin.

Suggested reading:

Ron Clark, *Setting the Captives Free*
Jackson Katz, *The Macho Paradox*
Al Miles, *Domestic Violence: What Every Pastor Needs to Know*
David Livingston, *Healing Violent Men*

Sixth year/cycle: Mentoring and Identifying Future Leaders

This cycle will be a time to develop mentoring relationships between elders and future elders, and elders' wives and other women. Mentoring is a lost art in Christianity. The books listed below place a strong emphasis on identifying faithful people and mentoring them. Both are good resources to read and discuss. The Pastorals will again be good biblical texts to use.

Suggested reading:

Howard and William Hendricks, *As Iron Sharpens Iron*

Edgar J. Elliston, *Home Grown Leaders*

I have given only a suggested training cycle for churches. This seems to follow a logical pattern while pulling the elders and students deeper into the biblical texts each cycle. The cycles can be repeated, or you can develop your own cycles. I feel that no more than thirteen to fifteen weeks should be spent on each cycle and no less than ten weeks. This will give everyone time to digest the reading material, but it will not extend the class into exhaustion or mental burnout (which happened our first year). It is a good idea for the classes to be sixty to ninety minutes with enough time allowed for homework. Currently this program can train elders/wives and potential elders/wives once per year for six years. New people can enter the program at any time and will learn as they go and can be mentored by the other leaders.

Make sure all elders are present and involved in the classes and discussions. Encourage the couples to spend time outside of class developing relationships with those just beginning the class. This is not supposed to be an academic class; it is supposed to involve lifelong relationships. Not only will people learn new material, they will develop solid relationships.

ENDNOTES

[1] Robert Richardson, *Principles of the Reformation*, edited by Carson E. Reed (Orange, CA: New Leaf Books, 2002): 97-98.

[2] Scott Thumma and Dave Travis, *Beyond Megachurch Myths* (San Francisco, CA: John Wiley and Sons, 2007), 55-56.

[3] See Leroy Garrett, *The Stone-Campbell Movement: An Anecdotal History of Three Churches*, 3rd printing (Joplin, MO: College Press, 1985), 1; and Henry E. Webb, *In Search of Christian Unity: A History of the Restoration Movement*, revised edition (Abilene: ACU Press, 2003), 9.

[4] Gary L. McIntosh. *One Size Doesn't Fit All* (Grand Rapids: Baker, 1999), 17.

[5] In my early doctoral work on these churches I used the title "transition churches," since these churches still had their roots and history in mutual ministry, but they had transitioned to the local preacher system.

[6] This movement was labeled the "Crossroads Movement," in its early stages since it began with the Crossroads Church of Christ. It later was called the "Discipling Movement," and then the "Boston Movement." The movement later called themselves the International Churches of Christ. For an excellent resource on the International Churches of Christ, see C. Foster Stanback, *Into all the Nations: A History of the International Churches of Christ* (Boston: Illumination Publication, 2005).

[7] Scott Green, "Effective Leadership," *Disciples Today* (March 13, 2006): 1, www.disciplestoday.net

[8] Ibid., 3.

[9] Guder, Darrell L., editor, *Missional Church: A Vision for the Sending of the Church in North America* (Grand Rapids: Eerdmans, 1998), 196.

[10] Ed Stetzer, *Planting New Churches in a Postmodern Age* (Nashville: Broadman and Holman, 2003), 140.

[11] John H. Elliott, "Ministry and Church Order in the NT: A Traditio-Historical Analysis," *Catholic Biblical Quarterly* 32:3 (2001): 368; Arthur G. Patzia., *The Emergence of the Church: Context, Growth, Leadership and Worship* (Downers Grove, IL: InterVarsity, 2001), 2-3; and Ritva H. Williams. *Stewards, Prophets, Keepers of the Word: Leadership in the Early Church* (Peabody, MA: Hendrickson, 2006), 2.

[12] Williams, 2.

[13] Paul and Barnabas began their mission trip about 47/48 AD. They would have returned to Antioch in 48/49 AD. Paul and Barnabas needed to be in Antioch by

48 AD in order to make the long trip to Corinth before 50 AD. This suggests that the churches in Galatia were one to one and a half years old when Paul and Barnabas returned on their way to Antioch (48/49 AD). I would suggest that elders were appointed in Syria around 49 AD. We traditionally would consider these elders to be newer converts to Christianity.

[14]It is important to realize that the Greek term for new convert (*neophyte*) is a new plant. A neophyte is more similar to a recently baptized individual.

[15]Bruce Winter, *Roman Wives, Roman Widows: The Appearance of New Women and the Pauline Community* (Grand Rapids: Eerdmans, 2003), 150.

[16]John Dominic Crossan, *God and Empire: Jesus Against Rome Then and Now* (New York: Harper Collins, 2007), 157-58.

[17]Proselytes are Gentiles who were converted to Judaism. This involved circumcision and, according to many historians, baptism.

[18]Robert Lewis and Rob Wilkins, *The Church of Irresistible Influence* (Grand Rapids: Zondervan, 2001), 157.

[19]Charles Arn, "A Response to Dr. Rainer," *Journal of the American Society for Church Growth*, vol. 6, 1995.

[20]Ed Stetzer and Philip Connor, Research Report: Church Plant Survivability and Health Study 2007 (Center For Missional Research, North American Mission Board, 2007).

[21]Tom Clegg and Warren Bird. *Lost in America* (Loveland, CO: Group Publishing, 2001).

[22]Ibid.

[23]Thom Rainer, *Kairos Church Planting Summit*, September 2005, St. Louis, MO.

[24]Ibid.

[25]Ibid.

[26]Ibid.

[27]Lewis, 17.

[28]Stanley Granberg. The Growth and Decline of the Churches of Christ in the United States: A Visual Review, 1980-200 www.kairoschurchplanting.org.

[29]McIntosh., 179.

[30]Lewis, 17.

[31]McIntosh, *Biblical Church Growth: How You Can Work with God to Build a Faithful Church* (Grand Rapids: Baker, 2003), 92.

[32]Rainer, *The Book of Church Growth: History, Theology, and Principles* (Nashville: Broadman, 1993), 186-91.

[33]McIntosh, 94.

[34]Lee Irons, "Theories of Eldership: A Study in Presbyterian Polity," page 5 www.upper-register.com/other_studies/eldership.html.

[35]Hanoch Reviv, *The Elders in Ancient Israel: A Study of a Biblical Institution*, translated by Lucy Plitmann (Jerusalem: Magnes Press, 1989), 189.

[36]Benjamin L. Merkle, *The Elder and Overseer: One Office in the Early Church* (NY: Peter Lang, 2003), 37-38.

[37]Ibid., 25.

[38]Reviv, 190.

[39]Timothy M. Willis, *The Elders of the City: A Study of the Elders-Laws in Deuteronomy* (Atlanta: Society of Biblical Literature, 2001), 307-08.

[40]Brian J. Dodd, *Empowered Church Leadership: Ministry in the Spirit According to Paul* (Downer's Grove, IL: InterVarsity Press, 2003), 16.

[41]Norman Shawchuck and Roger Heuser, *Leading the Congregation* (Nashville: Abingdon, 1993), 157-63, 210-15

[42]Frederick D. Aquino, "The Incarnation: The Dignity and Honor of Human Person-hood," *Restoration Quarterly* 42:1 (2000): 45.

[43]Neil Ormerod suggests that the mission of the church is to mediate God's grace and transform evil into good through three manifestations: personal, cultural, and social. Neil Ormerod, "System, History, and a Theology of Ministry," *Theological Studies* 61 (2000): 441-42. Phil Robinson suggests these mediations as levels of transformation in society: individual/personal, public/social, and deeper/cultural. Phil Robinson, "The Church in the Public Sphere: Some Perspectives from Matthew 5:13-16," *Missionalia* 25:3 (November 1997): 279.

[44]Gen. 50:24; Ex. 3:16; 4:31; Ps. 8:5; Jer. 23:2.

[45]Gen. 40:4; Num. 27:16; Neh. 7:1; Jer. 15:3.

[46]In a good way, Gen. 21:1; 50:24, 25; Ex. 13:19; Is. 23:17; Ezek. 38:8, or for punishment Ex. 20:5; 34:7; Deut. 5:9; Jer. 6:6; 9:24; 11:22; Hos. 1:4; 2:15; Amos 3:2, 14.

[47]Gen. 39:4; Num. 4:16; 2 Kings 25:23; Jer. 1:10; Ezek. 44:11. Brown, Driver and Briggs further give "take charge of" and "muster" as definitions of this word. Francis Brown, S.R. Driver, and Charles A. Briggs, *The New Brown-Driver-Briggs-Gesenius Hebrew and English Lexicon* (Peabody, MA: Hendrickson, 1979), 823-24 (hereafter cited as *BDB*). Koehler and Baumgartner also suggest that the word means an overseer, leader, and administrator. Ludwig Koehler and Walter Baumgartner, *The Hebrew and Aramaic Lexicon of the Old Testament, Vol. 3*, translated and edited by M.E.J. Richardson (New York: Brill, 1996), 960.

[48]The basic meaning of this term is "to exercise oversight over a subordinate, either in the form of inspecting or of taking action to cause a considerable change in the circumstances of the subordinate; for the better or for the worse." Harris also indicated that the term meant "to muster troops" and was used for soldiers, Levites, and priests. R. Laird Harris, *Theological Wordbook of the Old Testament*, vol. 2 (Chicago: Moody Press, 1980): 731. Overseers care for those who depend upon his support. This does not suggest abuse but compassion.

[49]I have noticed that over 85 percent of the time *episkopeo* or *episkope* is translated from a *pqd* root.

[50]*Episkopeo* meant to look at, take care of, or oversee. *Episkope* meant visitation or to be in a position to oversee. *Episkopos* meant overseer, guardian, or superintendent. The verb *Episkeptomai* meant to look for, look after, or be concerned about. Walter Bauer,

A Greek-English Lexicon of the New Testament and Other Early Christian Literature, 2d. ed., revised by William F. Arndt, F. Wilbur Gingrich, and Frederick W. Danker (Chicago: University of Chicago Press, 1979), 289-98 (hereafter cited as *BAG*).

[51]Ignatius, *Epistle to Polycarp*, 8:3; *Epistle to the Romans*, 9:1. *1 Clement*, 50:3; 59:3.

[52]Brown also defines *r'ah* as to look at, take a look, find out, provide or furnish, appear, or give attention to. *BDB*, 906-09.

[53]In the story of the attempted sacrifice of Isaac, the phrase traditionally translated as "God will provide" is actually "*Yahweh* sees."

[54]*Shamay* means to hear, listen, understand, obey, proclaim, report (verb and noun), and consent. *BDB*, 1033-35.

[55]The Hebrew terms for justice and righteousness in ancient Near Eastern contexts indicated social justice. See: J. Bazak, "The Meaning of the Terms 'Justice and Righteousness' in the Bible," *The Jewish Law Annual* 8 (1988): 5-18; and Moshe Weinfeld, *Social Justice in Ancient Israel and in the Ancient Near East* (Minneapolis: Fortress, 1995).

[56]C. K. Barrett, *A Critical and Exegetical Commentary on the Acts of the Apostles, vol. 2, The International Critical Commentary* (Edinburgh: T and T Clark, 1998), 975.

[57]"The ongoing ministry of Jesus Christ gives both content and direction to the church in its ministry. Jesus is the minister par excellence . . . Christ's primary ministry is to the Father for the sake of the world, not to the world for the sake of the Father." Ray S. Anderson, *The Shape of Practical Theology: Empowering Ministry with Theological Praxis* (Downer's Grove, IL: InterVarsity Press, 2001), 62-63.

[58]James D. Whitehead and Evelyn Eaton Whitehead, *The Promise of Partnership* (San Francisco: Harper, 1991), 29, 59-60.

[59]Walther Eichrodt, *Theology of the Old Testament*, Vol. 1, trans. by J. A. Baker, *Old Testament Library* (Philadelphia: Westminster, 1961), 37.

[60]Ibid., 37. Renita J. Weems discusses the unfaithful wife metaphor in the prophets as a relationship between God and Israel that was marked by mutual obligations and mutual responsibilities. Renita J. Weems, *Battered Love*, in Overtures to Biblical Theology (Minneapolis: Fortress Press, 1995), 17.

[61]Eichrodt, 37, 38.

[62]All Biblical references in this paper are taken from the New International Version. All Hebrew texts are taken from *Biblia Hebraica Stuttgartensia*, ed. Karl Elliger and Wilhelm Rudolph (Stuttgart: Deutsche Biblestiftung, 1977). All Greek texts are taken from *Novum Testamentum Graece*, 27th ed., ed. Eberhard Nestle, Erwin Nestle, Barbara Aland, Kurt Aland, Johannes Karavidopoulos, Carlo M. Martini, Bruce M. Metzger (Stuttgart: Deutsche Bibelgesellschaft, 1993). .

[63]Brown suggests that the term for shepherd is similar to friend. The term does suggest relationship. *BDB*, 944-45. J. G. S. S. Thomson, "The Shepherd-Ruler Conception in the Old Testament and Its Application in the New Testament," *Scottish Journal of Theology* 8:4 (December 1955): 406. Thomson indicates that ancient use of shepherd was used to describe a relationship between a ruler or king and his people. This

relationship involved compassion and respect. Zimmerli writes that the stock term for king was "shepherd" or "good shepherd" in Sumerian, Akkadian, Assyrian, Babylonian, Egyptian, and other ancient Near Eastern literature. See Walther Zimmerli, *Ezekiel 2: A Commentary on the Book of the Prophet Ezekiel, Chapters 24-48*, in Hermeneia, trans. Ronald E. Clements (Philadelphia: Fortress, 1983), 213.

[64]Ian Fair, *Leadership in the Kingdom*, (Abilene: ACU Press, 1996), 37-50, 108, 325-27.

[65]Bernie Crum, interview by author, tape recording, Park Hills, MO, 12 July 1997; Jim Mabery, interview by author, tape recording, Hot Springs Village, AR, 25 June 1997; and Jerry Ketcherside, interview by author, tape recording, Hot Springs Village, AR, 25 June 1997. Concerning a modern move in the denominations regarding elder-based leadership, see Stanley J. Grenz, "Is Elder Rule a Threat?" *Christianity Today* 31:9 (10 July 1987): 48, 50.

[66]Vision has three dimensions: an upward view of God, an inward view of the self, and an outward view of the circumstances. Shawchuck and Heuser, 71.

[67]R. N. Whybray, *Proverbs*, in The New Century Bible Commentary (Grand Rapids: Eerdmans, 1994), 386. The shepherd is relational in that he knows the "face of the flock" and is blessed by the produce of the flock (clothing and milk). Whybray, 387. Knowing the flocks' life history, background, and conditions of the flock helps the elders shepherd the church so that they can be blessed by a congregation that is walking with God (Heb. 13:17 the leader's work is a joy rather than a burden). Claude Cox writes that a person's life history is valuable in pastoral care and allows us to intersect into their world. Claude Cox, "The Importance of Lifestory in Pastoral Care," *Restoration Quarterly* 38:8 (1996): 108, 116, 120.

[68]Ibid.

[69]Usually the word *peitho* is translated "obey," but I see that it means "persuaded." Timothy Willis, "'Obey Your Leaders': Hebrews 13 and Leadership in the Church," *Restoration Quarterly* 36:4 (1994): 316-26.

[70]Bauer indicates that *diakonos* is a servant, helper, deacon, or agent, and the verb *diakoneo* suggests service, to care for, and to help. *BAG*, 184. *Diakonos* can mean "an agent" or "to act as a go-between." See J. N. Collins, *Diakonia: Re-interpreting the Ancient Sources* (New York: Oxford University Press, 1990), 191, 336; Collins indicates that *diakonos* is not limited to "service" but means acting as a "go-between" or fulfilling an administrative role.

[71]In team ministry, each member is part of the whole body, working together to contribute to the growth and development of the church. Eph. 4:11-16 indicates that team ministry works to fulfill the commission given to the apostles, which includes training others for good works (Mt. 28:18-20; Tit. 2:14; Eph. 2:10). Fair, 190-91; Stephen R. Covey, *Principle-Centered Leadership* (New York: Summit Books, 1991); Robert C. DeVries, "Structuring the Multiple-Staff Ministry," *Team Ministry* (Grand Rapids: CRC Publications, 1988), 29-35; Joseph T. Kelly, "Five Group Dynamics in Team Ministry," *The Journal of Pastoral Care* 48 (Summer 1994): 118-30; and Whitehead, 104.

[72]J. A. Thompson, *The Book of Jeremiah*, The New International Commentary on the Old Testament (Grand Rapids: Eerdmans, 1980), 406.

[73]Fowler, *Faith Development and Pastoral Care*, Theology and Pastoral Care Series, ed. Don S. Browning (Philadelphia: Fortress, 1987), 21. Leaders cannot assume that church attendance is sufficient to develop Christian faith. Maurice Ryan and William J. Foster, "Mass Attendance and Faith Development in Catholic Adolescents: Exploring Connections," *Journal of Christian Education* 38 (April 1995): 47-57, suggest that an increase or decrease in church attendance does not indicate a shift in the dynamics of one's faith relationship. See also Kenneth Stokes, "Faith Development in the Adult Life Cycle," *Journal of Religious Gerontology* 7:1/2 (1990): 167-84.

[74]Since Paul addressed the Philippian letter to the "bishops and deacons," I believe that he expected these leaders to take responsibility for helping the two women (Phil. 1:1; 4:2). Notice Paul's challenge to "work out their own salvation with fear and trembling" (2:12).

[75]Winter claims that Paul wanted the Corinthian Christians to avoid court because it involved shaming one's opponent with the abuses from lawyers and judges. Bruce W. Winter, *After Paul Left Corinth: The Influence of Secular Ethics and Social Change* (Grand Rapids: Eerdmans, 2001), 58-75. David deSilva suggests that Roman and Greek authors also claimed that patrons were to exhibit friendship and grace in their relationships with subordinates. This would support Paul's suggestion that they work out issues among themselves (2:12; 4:2). David A. deSilva, *Honor, Patronage, Kinship, and Purity* (Downer's Grove, IL: InterVarsity Press, 2001), 96-99.

[76]Weems, 89-93.

[77]Robert Sutton, "By Invitation: Building a Civilized Workplace," The McKinsey Quarterly (2007) 2: 47-55.

[78]Amy G. Oden, *And You Welcomed Me: A Sourcebook on Hospitality in Early Christianity* (Nashville: Abingdon, 2001), 14-16. Hospitality in the Greco-Roman culture was practiced as a method of gaining favors in the patron/client system of the culture. Men would have clients as their servants or debtors who spent much of their time paying back favors by giving honor and praise to their "patrons." Hospitality was necessary in order for the head of the family (*patria familia*) to continue to be respected by the people. deSilva, 95-119; Halvor Moxnes, "What is Family: Problems in Constructing Early Christian Families," *Constructing Early Christian Families: Family as Social Reality and Metaphor* (New York: Routledge, 1997), 26; and Carolyn Osiek and David L. Balch, *Families in the New Testament World: Households and House Churches* (Louisville: Westminster/John Knox, 1997), 39.

[79]Ibid., 15.

[80]Notice that Paul encourages the church to associate with the humble (*tapeinois*) rather than be proud. See my article "Associating with the Humiliated," *Journal of Religion and Abuse* 7:1 (2005):12-20.

[81]For more on the dynamics of abuse, power, and control, see my book: *Setting the Captives Free: A Christian Theology for Domestic Violence* (Eugene, OR: Cascade Books, 2005).

[82]J. Jeffrey Means, *Trauma and Evil: Healing the Wounded Soul* (Minneapolis: Fortress, 2000), 16, 24.

[83]The leaders are called shepherds in light of the ancient Near Eastern tradition of referring to kings and officials as shepherds. Thomson, 406, Zimmerli, 213, and G. A. Cooke, *A Critical and Exegetical Commentary on the Book of Ezekiel*, in The International Critical Commentary (Edinburgh: T. & T. Clark, 1985), 373.

[84]Greenberg indicates that eating the fat (translated curds in some versions) suggested that the leaders were living off of the people. The term for fat indicates a delicacy (Gen. 45:18 for fat/best of the land) and was that part of the animal burned and given to God. The Israelite leaders were evidently living well while the people suffered. Moshe Greenberg, *Ezekiel 21-48*, in The Anchor Bible Commentary (Garden City, NY: Doubleday, 1997), 696.

[85]It seems that the major points are that the shepherds have *ruled harshly and brutally* by *not shepherding the sheep or binding the broken ones* (Zimmerli, 215). They have abused the sheep out of selfishness (34:3a) and neglected them (34:3b-4). In Ezek. 34:16 God promises, in reverse order from 34:4, to seek the perishing, turn back the lost, bind the broken, strengthen the injured, destroy the sleek and strong, and shepherd with justice. In the middle of this section God promises to gather and return the people back to the fold (v7-10) by vindicating the sheep and confronting and removing the shepherds from their position. He will search for the sheep and shepherd them justly.

[86]Greenberg suggests that they ruled with force (Lev. 25:43, 46, 53; Judg. 4:3). Ibid., 697. Zimmerli believes that "brutality" is a better translation of *pqd*. Zimmerli, 215.

[87]The mention of hills and mountains indicates a major concern of *Yahweh* for his sheep. The "high hills" may refer to Israel's wandering into Canaanite idolatry (6:13; 18:6, 20:28). In this text Israel's forsaking God is a direct result of bad or inattentive shepherding. "The exile is the bitter fruit of the bad shepherding in which no one really sought or cared for His flock." Zimmerli, 215. Greenberg suggests that *stray* could indicate moral and physical sin (Ps. 119:10) or erring unwittingly (Lev. 4:13; Num. 15:22; Ezek. 45:20). Greenberg, 698.

[88]This text echoes God's condemnation also found in Jer. 23:2 where God blames the shepherds for the wandering sheep. The use of the Hebrew verb suggests an intense translation "chased" the sheep away. William L. Holladay, *A Commentary on the Book of the Prophet Jeremiah, Chapters 1-25*, in *Hermeneia* (Philadelphia: Fortress, 1986), 614. Thompson suggests that the two uses of *pqd* in 23:2 indicate that since the shepherds have not paid attention to the flock, God would call them to accountability. He indicates that God will hold them accountable, rather than watch over them. J. A.

Thompson, *The Book of Jeremiah*, in the New International Commentary on the Old Testament (Grand Rapids: Eerdmans, 1980), 487.

[89]Zimmerli indicates that the three-fold use of the stem for *pqd* suggests a "careful and painstaking examination of the circumstances given in the respective context." He also points out that the old Nabatean *mbqr* was a title of an official who closely observed the animal sacrifice. Zimmerli, 216.

[90]Weinfeld, 67.

[91]I think the use of feed and lambs suggests a more personal relationship between the shepherd and sheep. Peter was not just told to shepherd sheep but to feed the lambs.

[92]J. Ramsey Michaels, *1 Peter*, The Word Biblical Commentary, vol. 49 (Waco, TX: Word, 1988), 382. Michaels also mentions that this section (5:1-4) follows the warning that judgment begins with the family of God (4:17).

[93]Notice that Paul also uses this word in Philm. 14. Peter suggests that they practice hospitality without complaining (1 Peter 4:9). Martin also indicates that Peter's call to humility may also suggest to the elders a strong relationship with the sheep or the humble. Troy W. Martin, *Metaphor and Composition in 1 Peter*, SBL Dissertation Series 131 (Atlanta: Scholars, 1992), 261.

[94]Paul also warns elders about being greedy (1 Tim. 3:8; Tit. 1:7). See Martin, 260.

[95]Michaels, 282-85.

[96]Barrett writes that this word suggests that the elders have been singled out by the Holy Spirit by being gifted for shepherding and oversight. "The ministry is not appointed from below, nor from above if this means by those already ministers; the Holy Spirit is at work in the church choosing and preparing by his gifts those who are to be ministers. The Holy Spirit appointed them in order that they might shepherd ... God's flock." Barrett, 974-75.

[97]Andrew D. Clarke, *First-Century Christians in the Graeco-Roman World: Serve the Community of the Church: Christians as Leaders and Ministers* (Grand Rapids: Eerdmans, 2000), 11-58.

[98]I agree with Fair, 292, and Anderson, 130-31, who suggest that this is not a good way to interpret these texts and apply them to modern elders.

[99]Marshall, 482. Mounce believes that the church began ten years earlier than the writing of this letter. Mounce, 181.

[100]Perry L. Stepp, *Leadership Succession in the World of the Pauline Circle* (Sheffield, England: Sheffield Phoenix, 2005), 138.

[101]Mounce, 181.

[102]Stepp, 138.

[103]George W. Knight III, *The Pastoral Epistles: A Commentary on the Greek Text*, New International Greek Testament Commentary (Grand Rapids: Eerdmans, 1996), 161. Mounce, 179.

[104]For more on Proverbs and scribal schools see my article: "Schools, Scribes, and Scholars: The Wisdom School *Sitz ImLeben* and Proverbs," *Restoration Quarterly* 47:3 (2005): 161-77.

[105]Craig de Vos gives an indication about the social and cultural relationships that Christians would have had in the Greco-Roman world. The Roman culture had a strong affinity between government and religious practice. Most of the clubs and civic organizations required the leaders to be priestly in their nature concerning sacrifices and libations to their chosen god. This gave them permission to assemble, worship, and practice their faith legally. Craig Steven de Vos, *Church and Community Conflicts: The Relationships of the Thessalonian, Corinthian, and Philippian Churches within Their Wider Civic Community*, SBL Dissertation Series, 168 (Atlanta: Scholars, 1997).

[106]Mounce lists a comparison between the Pastoral qualities of leaders and the moral nature of the opponents to the church. It seems that Paul is directly challenging the character of the opponents by calling the elders, and church, to an ethical standard. Mounce, 156-58.

[107]Bauer, 65; Marshall, 477.

[108]There is a strong debate on the meaning of this phrase. Mounce, 171-73; Knight, 157-58; and Marshall, 478, suggest that the elder is one who is married and that the phrase is a general indication of his faithfulness. Dibelius and Conzelmann seem to indicate that this does not apply to the bishop in general. Martin Dibelius and Hans Conzelmann, *A Commentary on the Pastoral Epistles*, trans. Philip Buttolph and Adela Yarbro, ed. Helmut Koester, Hermeneia (Philadelphia: Fortress, 1972), 52.

[109]Keith R. Bradley, "Remarriage and the Structure of the Upper-Class Roman Family," *Marriage, Divorce, and Children in Ancient Rome*, ed. Beryl Rawson (Clarendon: Oxford, 1991), 85; Susan Treggiari, "Divorce Roman Style: How Easy and How Frequent Was It?" *Marriage, Divorce, and Children in Ancient Rome*, ed. Beryl Rawson (Clarendon: Oxford, 1991), 35.

[110]Winter, 160-61.

[111]Bauer gives the definition at the head of, rule, direct, be concerned about, care for, give aid, engage in, or busy oneself. Bauer, 707. Reicke suggests to go first, protect, and lead. Bo Reicke, *"prohistemi,"* in *Theological Dictionary of the New Testament*, ed. Gerhard Friedrich, trans. and ed. Geoffrey W. Bromiley (Grand Rapids: Eerdmans, 1973), 6:700-703.

[112]Williams, 55.

[113]Ibid., 57.

[114]For a fuller explanation of this, see my article, Clark, "Family Management or Involvement? Paul's Use of proïsthmi in 1 Timothy 3:4,5,12 as a Requirement for Church Leadership," *Stone Campbell Journal* 9:2 (2006): 243-52.

[115]"There are hardly any people who wield as much power over their sons as we do." Gaius, *Institutes*, 557. Eyben indicates that the father's right to expose infants, and scourge, sell, pawn, and imprison or kill his son at any time has led to the belief that

fathers were cruel and harsh. Yet many fathers did not practice these rights. Eyben, 115.

[116]Suzanne Dixon, *The Roman Family* (Baltimore: Johns Hopkins University, 1992), 100, 116. See also Richard Saller, "Corporal Punishment, Authority, and Obedience in the Roman Household," *Marriage, Divorce, and Children in Ancient Rome*, ed. Beryl Rawson (Clarendon: Oxford, 1991), 161-62.

[117]Sir. 30:7-13. All quotes from the Apocrypha are from the New Revised Standard Version Bible.

[118]Ibid., 116-17, 131.

[119]See Keith R. Bradley's chapter "Child Care at Rome: The Role of Men," in *Discovering the Roman Family* (New York: Oxford, 1991), 37-75.

[120]"It was clearly usual for elite children to grow up surrounded by a variety of such caregivers, especially in early childhood." Dixon, *Roman Family*, 119.

[121]Jeffers, 141; and David C. Verner, *The Household of God: The Social World of the Pastoral Epistles*, SBL Dissertation Series, vol. 71, ed. William Baird (Chico, CA: Scholars Press, 1983), 31, 68-70.

[122]"The male householder, then, functioned both as the representative of his *domus/oikos* . . . and as the agent of his household's subordination to the loftier goals of the city." Bartchy also writes that the honor of the *paterfamilias* was dependent upon his ability to protect his *domus*. S. Scott Bartchy, "Families in the Greco-Roman World," *The Family Handbook*, ed. Herbert Anderson, Don S. Browning, Ian S. Evison, and Mary Stewart Van Leeuwen (Louisville: Westminster/John Knox, 1998), 282-83. Submission and respect in the *domus/oikos* was necessary for the father to maintain honor and prove his effectiveness in ruling the city. Moxnes, 28.

[123]Bartchy, 284.

[124]Since the Philippian letter is written to "the bishops and deacons" (Phil. 1:1), I am assuming that they, as Christian leaders, were expected to follow Paul's suggestions. They may have been the ones who were "walking according to the pattern that you have from us" (3:17).

[125]Barth, 429, mentions that the Messiah is the gift which is given downward from God to Christ to man.

[126]Eager to keep the unity of the Spirit and the shared bond of peace (4:3). Lincoln, 237; Barth, 428.

[127]Porter wrote that *katallasso* in Greek literature was used in various contexts but that the main emphasis taken by Paul was reconciliation: Eph. 2:16, Jesus brings Jew and Gentile together, under the will of God. Stanley E. Porter, *Katallasso in Ancient Greek Literature, with Reference to the Pauline Writings*, Estudious de Filologia Neotestamentaria, 5 (Cordoba, Spain: Ediciones El Almendro, 1994), 185-89.

[128]Bauer, 417-18. Barth suggests restore. Barth, 439. Schnackenburg suggests encouragement and strengthening. Rudolf Schnackenburg, *The Epistle to the Ephesians: A Commentary*, trans. by Helen Heron (Edinburgh: T. and T. Clark, 1991), 183.

[129]Barth, 439-40; Schnackenburg, 183. Both authors do believe that it refers to the service of the saints.

[130]Schnackenberg, 183.

[131]Barth suggests that this means building up the Messiah's body. Barth, 440. Lincoln and Davies make a separation between ministry from leaders (ministers) and members. Lincoln, 255; John Jefferson Davies, "Ephesians 4:12 Once More: 'Equipping the Saints for the Work of Ministry?" *Evangelical Reformed Theology* 24:2 (2000): 170-2.

[132]Mature person or adult. Schnackenburg, 185; Lincoln, 256.

[133]Ibid., 256.

[134]Cole, 134-35.

[135]We have traditionally accepted the translation of 1 Cor. 13:8 as "that which is perfect" because we have believed that this referred to Jesus or the completed Bible. "That which is mature" is a better translation because Paul is telling the church to grow up and mature. In 1 Cor. 13, he discusses how he acted as a child but as he became a man he put away childish things. Tongues edify the person, which Paul would say is not an act of *agape*, or that which is mature.

[136]I understand that most of our English texts translate this word as obey. In Greek culture, efficient leaders were able to persuade people. In our culture, which is similar to Roman culture, we seem to stress obedience. The Hebrew word for obedience and listen are the same (*shamay*). In an oral culture, obedience was displayed in a willingness to first listen and then respond. But the gap between the command/statement and response was affected by the speaker's character and ability to persuade the hearer to choose to respond.

[137]Bruce Tulgan, *It's OK to Be the Boss* (New York: Harper Collins, 2007).

[138]Frost and Ala Hirsch, 39-41; Stetzer, 189-95.

[139] Alan Hirsch, *The Forgotten Ways* (Grand Rapids: Brazos, 2007), 133.

[140]Ibid., 267-8.

[141]Clark, "Schools," 162-63.

[142]Michael J. Wilkins, *Discipleship in the Ancient World and Matthew's Gospel*, 2nd ed. (Grand Rapids: Baker, 1995), 21-25.

[143]deSilva, 95-98.

[144]Lutz, 32-33.

[145]Thomas H. Olbricht, "*Pathos* As Proof in Greco-Roman Rhetoric," *Paul and Pathos*, ed. Thomas H. Olbircht and Jerry L. Sumney, SBL Symposium Series 16 (Atlanta: Society of Biblical Literature, 2001), 8-22.

[146]Stepp, 138.

[147]Williams, 57.

[148]Joseph H. Hellerman, *The Ancient Church as Family* (Minneapolis: Augsburg Fortress, 2001), 1-3.

[149]Great reading materials on this issue are Philip A. Harland, *Associations, Synagogues, and Congregations: Claiming a Place in Ancient Mediterranean Society* (Minneapolis:

Augsburg Fortress, 2003); and Dennis E. Smith, *From Symposium to Eucharist: The Banquet in the Early Christian World* (Minneapolis: Augsburg Fortress, 2003), 1-12.

[150]Stepp, 111-152; Christopher R. Hutson, "'Exercise Yourself in Piety:' 1 Timothy 4 as a Training Regimen for Young Servants of Christ," *Christian Scholar's Conference*, Abilene Christian University, July 17-19, 1997, Abilene, TX; and 2 Tim. 3:10.

[151]R. Murray Thomas, *Moral Development Theories—Secular and Religious: A Comparative Study* (Westport, CT: Greenwood Press, 1997). James W. Fowler, *Weaving the New Creation* (San Francisco: Harper Collins, 1991), 57-65.

[152] Ibid.,91-92, 101-03.

[153]Donald R. Ploch and Donald W. Hasitings, *Review of Religious Research* 39 (June 1998). For more on family and faith formation, see Roland D. Martinson, "The Role of Family in the Faith and Value Formation of Children," *Word and World* 17 (Fall 1997): 396-404.

[154]Kwilecki, 234.

[155]Judith K. TenElshof and James L. Furrow, "The Role of Secure Attachment in Predicting Spiritual Maturity of Students at a Conservative Seminary" *Journal of Psychology and Theology* 28:2 (2000): 99-108.

[156]Winter, *After Paul Left Corinth: The Influence of Secular Ethics and Social Change* (Grand Rapids: Eerdmans, 2001), 31-43; Ben Witherington III, *Conflict and Community in Corinth: A Socio-Rhetorical Commentary on 1 and 2 Corinthians* (Grand Rapids: Eerdmans, 1995), 151-62.

[157]Craig Steven, de Vos, *Church and Community Conflicts: The Relationships of the Thessalonian, Corinthian, and Philippian Churches with Their Wider Civic Communities*, SBL Dissertation Series 168 (Atlanta: Scholars Press, 1999), 179-232.

[158]For more on life story and shepherding see Claude Cox, "The Importance of Lifestory in Pastoral Care," *Restoration Quarterly* 38:2 (1996): 109-20.

[159]Ronald W. Richardson, *Creating a Healthier Church: Family Systems Theory, Leadership, and Congregational Life,* Creative Pastoral Care and Counseling Series (Minneapolis: Fortress, 1996). This is an excellent resource for those wishing to help a church heal as a system.

[160]Ibid., 49-50.

[161]My work with the Oregon Attorney General's Sexual Assault Task Force exposes me to current research in sexual assault. The FBI and other national task force organizations have given compelling evidence that false allegations are not typically false, but reports recanted due to pressure and stress on the victim. Victims are usually chosen because they are seen as lacking credibility.

[162]A powerful survey of men has recently been published for men in the churches of Christ. John Bentley, *The Problem of Internet Pornography* (Feb. 8, 2005) available at jbentley@campbellstreet.org

[163]Clark, *Setting the Captives Free*, xvi-xvii.

[164]Alberto Gonzales, Regina B. Schofield, and Glenn R. Schmitt, *Sexual Assault on Campuses: What Colleges and Universities are Doing About It* (Washington, DC: U.S. Department of Justice, 2005) http://www.oregonsatf.org/documents/SACampus2005.pdf.

[165]For more on this story and the scholarly debate about whether or not Dinah was raped, see my article, Ron Clark, "The Silence in Dinah's Cry," *Lectio Difficilior* 1:2006 (www.lectio.unibe.ch/06_1/clark_silence.htm); and *Restoration Quarterly* 49:3 (2007): 143-58.

[166]David Goetz, "Why Pastor Steve Loves His Job." *Christianity Today* 41:4 (April 7, 1997): 12-19.

[167]An excellent resource that discusses many of the potential negative issues ministers face as leaders is: Gary L. McIntosh and Samuel D. Rima, Sr., *Overcoming the Dark Side of Leadership: The Paradox of Personal Dysfunction* (Grand Rapids: Baker, 2004).

[168]Candace R. Benyei, *Understanding Clergy Misconduct in Religious Systems: Scapegoating, Family Secrets, and the Abuse of Power* (New York: Haworth Press, 1998), 37.

[169] Roy M. Oswald and Otto Kroeger, *Personality Type and Religious Leadership* (Herndon, VA: Alban Institute, 1999), 128-29.

[170]Two excellent books that have challenged me concerning the newer generation's view of social justice, church growth, and Jesus illustrate well the need for our churches to engage this culture. See Shane Claiborne, *The Irresistible Revolution: Living as an Ordinary Radical* (Grand Rapids: Zondervan, 2006), and Neil Cole, *Organic Church: Growing Faith Where Life Happens* (San Francisco: Jossey-Bass, 2005).

[171]Resources on Luke/Acts bring tremendous light on the social justice of Jesus. Jesus called us to free the oppressed (Luke 4:18-19).

ACKNOWLEDGEMENTS

This book was a project that began in 1996. The Bonne Terre Church Christ in Missouri helped me to attend graduate school and work with the idea of elder development. The project originally began as an exploration of the Mutual Ministry movement but later progressed to an elder development ministry after I moved to Oregon. The Metro Church of Christ in Gresham became our first "test case" as one of the elders, Doug Davis, and I began classes and training for men. Over the next eight years many men and women attended training sessions and eight couples stepped into the role as shepherds. During this time I completed my doctorate in ministry at Harding Graduate School and finished my dissertation on developing elders in congregations. Through recent years this work seemed to be a needed resource and now, with this book, I hope it will serve as a training guide for elders and their wives, ministers, missionaries, and educators seeking to step into this responsibility.

I would like to thank both congregations that helped in the beginnings of these projects. The Bonne Terre Church of Christ and Metro Church of Christ have been great supporters in the area of leadership development. Thanks also go out to the many couples that attended training sessions in Portland, Oregon, and Toluca, Mexico. Doug Davis has been a great encouragement and model for me as both an elder and friend who seeks to develop other men. Mike Chandler, currently my mentor while a church planter, also has been a great supporter. Mike claims he would never have been an elder without this program but I think he and his wife Sharon have had it in them all the time. The couples, in addition to Doug and Barbara and Mike and Sharon, who have been through the training and shepherded for many years also deserve thanks: Shannon and Patty Sue Poole, John and Donna Heck, Mark and Janie Ellingson, Ron and Lianna Frunk, and David and Christie Vaca.

I am also indebted to Dr. Evertt Huffard who walked with me through the dissertation process. He has also been a great friend through years of ministry. I must also acknowledge the late James and Lee Mabery who mentored me in my early years of ministry. They embodied many of the characteristics of ministry and leadership development found in the Mutual Ministry and Mainline churches. They also taught me more about evangelism and people than I could have ever learned in school. Their fingerprints are numerous on the ministry Lori and I have developed over the years. They have also given us happy memories in both their marriage and ministry.

A note of thanks also goes out to the men who gave input and advice as I prepared this book for publication. These men are Lynn Anderson of Hope Network, Al Baird of the Los Angeles International Church of Christ, Scott Greene from the Seattle International Church of Christ, Steve Staten from the Chicago International Church of Christ, Bob Bertalot from the Portland International Church of Christ, Jack Coffee and John Foster from the Southeast Christian Church in Louisville, Stan Granberg of Kairos Church Planting, Don Millican from the Park Plaza Church of Christ in Tulsa, and Rodger Curtis from the East County Church of Christ in Portland. Your comments have all been both encouraging and enlightening. I have learned much from all of you and appreciate the time and energy you gave to reading the many rough drafts and communicating what needed to be said. Together I hope that we have written a useful resource for churches and leaders.

I would like to express my appreciation to Sue Tester who has been a faithful proofreader of my books. She does this for a Starbucks card. This time she worked through the manuscript while undergoing chemotherapy. The Lord is good and has healed her and our prayers have been answered

Finally, I want to give my heartfelt appreciation to Lori and the boys. Lori, one day we may serve in this role, and I know you and I will continue to make a great team. You are my ministry partner and best friend and much of this would not be possible without you. You help me see people in ways I have neglected for many years. You also help keep ministry and our work with people enjoyable. Nathan, Hunter, and Caleb: thank you for teaching me patience and empathy, and I hope that you will one day be able to use this in your service to God.

Ron Clark
Agape Church of Christ
Portland, Oregon
www.agapecoc.com

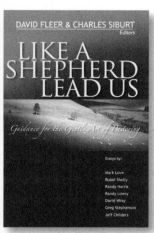
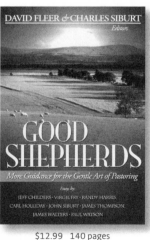

The Story of Churches of Christ

With a new Study Guide

GARY HOLLOWAY
& DOUGLAS A. FOSTER

RENEWING
GOD'S PEOPLE
A Concise History of Churches of Christ

WITH A NEW STUDY GUIDE

"**Renewing God's People** *will become the standard text for passing down our history to the next generation.*"

—Thomas H. Olbricht, author of *Hearing God's Voice*

176 pages $14.99
ISBN 0-89112-010-6

"*There has rarely been a time when Churches of Christ have so needed to read and study a book like this one by Foster and Holloway. It is a fresh and fair treatment of the American heritage of Churches of Christ and their distinctive plea for New Testament Christianity. It is well designed for either serious study and discussion by classes or for casual, personal reading. Everyone would do well to read and think about this important book.*"

—Lynn McMillon, Dean, College of Biblical Studies,
 Oklahoma Christian University

Abilene Christian University Press

To order call toll free 1-877-816-4455
Or visit our website: www.abilenechristianuniversitypress.com
Or ask for it at your favorite bookstore